SEX, DRUG'S

and a
Buddhist
Monk

SEX, DRUGS
and a
Buddhist Monk

A STEPPING STONE TOWARDS A SILENT MIND

LUKE KENNEDY

A Gelding Street Press book
An imprint of Rockpool Publishing, Pty Ltd
PO Box 252
Summer Hill
NSW 2130
Australia

www.geldingstreetpress.com

ISBN: 9781922579218

Published in 2022 by Gelding Street Press
Copyright text © Luke Kennedy 2022

Edited by Lisa Macken
Design by Sara Lindberg, Rockpool Publishing

 A catalogue record for this book is available from the National Library of Australia

Printed and bound in China
10 9 8 7 6 5 4 3 2 1

CONTENTS

Chapter 1

THE LOUD MIND

I don't want to do this. What if they've got weapons too? I might get locked up. I might get . . .

'Punchy, how much do you think they'll have?' my old friend Stintz asked me, seated next to me in the driver's seat of a stolen car, his words interrupting my inner thoughts. Punchy, my nickname, I had picked up through graffiti and winning organised street fights. I loved it.

'I'm not sure, bro. Don't know about cash, but they'll have heaps of pills,' my mouth spat out, trying to drown the other conversation in my head: my doubt and my fears. My thoughts were always there, always loud.

Those loud thoughts were the reason I was sitting in that car about to run through a drug dealer's house to rob him and his friends.

A couple of hours earlier I had been sitting on a warm couch with a bunch of my boys, the morning sun peeping through gaps in the curtains. It was the end of the second night without any sleep but with copious amounts of ecstasy, cocaine and alcohol.

Time on drugs gave me what I was after: a slight reprieve from my overactive mind. It gave me some stillness, some silent time. It helped me care less about what other people thought of me – at least, for a short time.

As the effects started to wear off and the misery of my harsh reality began to hit, my loud berserk thoughts were back in full force. And they were worse than before I got on the drugs.

Shouldn't have said that last night. You reckon they'll care?

Fuck, I'm going to be sick tomorrow . . . Should I have something to eat? When did I eat last? Ummm . . . wonder if I've lost weight.

I'm gunna go home. Fuck going home. Everyone else is still going.

How's my face look? I bet it's oily. I haven't showered in a bit. Do the boys think I'm a grub? Have they showered? Wouldn't mind brushing my teeth.

How can we get more drugs? Fuck, I need more drugs. Any vodka left? I think I finished it all off.

I was facing reality as the drugs wore off, and these thoughts were crawling their way back in. I didn't want the thoughts back.

How can I hold these thoughts back a little longer?

'Anyone got pills? Have we finished the vodka?' I slurred, glancing around the room filled with pale, miserable faces, purple bags sitting under every single defeated eye. There was no response besides a couple of weak and beaten shakes of the head.

2

The room had three lounges in a semi-circle, a large-screen TV playing music videos and a coffee table with empty beer bottles on top, a bong, empty satchels and a bloody tissue after two of the boys had a drunken wrestle a few hours earlier and butted heads. The jovial atmosphere of the night before had disappeared with the darkness of night. What was left was misery, the sun's rays now illuminating our horrible existence. One of the boys was slouched down into the couch, his head below his shoulders and giving the impression he had no neck.

'Fuck . . . wouldn't mind a pill,' was all he could mumble.

One of the other boys who had been in the wrestle the night before chuckled and coughed, a bit of blood-stained tissue still stuck on his head.

'Anyone got pills?' I repeated a little louder.

'Think we're done, brother,' Stintz said, disclosing the information we were all trying to hide from.

I had met Stintz four years earlier when he was 15 and I was 17. He was an innocent little skater boy back then, a young boy with an underlying mental health issue. He too was searching for stillness. He also craved silence.

With years of being in Sydney's most infamous graffiti and street-fighting crew, Stintz's defence, or more like attack, of the manic mind was to not only bury it in substance abuse but to also crush it down through adrenaline-filled, life on the edge experiences. Not skydiving or swimming with sharks, mind you; more like bursting into a business, jumping the counter, throwing an employee to the ground and robbing them. Or, like me, he also enjoyed a fight. He looked up to me. When I first met him he was a short kid with blond hair who was looking for guidance. Now four years later and still a touch shorter than me, he had broad shoulders, a thick neck with tattoos hugging it and many scars on his beaten face. He also had a team of younger people who looked up to him and did harsh acts at his request – the vicious cycle of gang life. You either fight your way to the top or you're left at the bottom doing things for those above you. Once at the top it's your turn to call the shots.

'Punchy, do you think I could beat him, he's a big boy?' Stintz asked me a few months after I first met him. There was an older guy from a rival crew who had called Stintz out. People in our crew never backed down, even if it meant a possible defeat.

'Brother, he might be big, but his heart is nowhere near yours.'

'With you in my corner, Punchy, I'll take on anyone.'

'I'll always be in your corner, my man.'

I was the main fighter in the crew. As I had grown up around the boxing scene and in a family of fighters – my dad and brother were both professional boxers – I won all of my street fights bar one.

I started my downward spiral after getting kicked out of school at 15. When I met the now-infamous graffiti crew RM I fought my way into it. I saw the way my dad and brother were looked up to: fighters were like gladiators in our circle. They deserved respect. I wanted that respect.

I just went about it the wrong way.

Years of organised street fights, getting stabbed twice – once in the lung and the other time in the head – and an unrelenting approach to gaining recognition meant I soon saw myself at the top of the crew.

I was happy to be labelled a fighter and leader. Again, I saw this as being like an ancient gladiator and it gave me a false sense of power. It gave me an identity, one that helped me feign confidence. In front of the boys I was this big, strong leader. I could handle any situation and wouldn't back down to anyone. I even looked happy.

Internally, though, it couldn't have been further from the truth. I was anxious, depressed and paranoid, and a lot of nights I would cry myself to sleep after praying to be a better man. In social situations away from the false confidence of gang life I was incredibly awkward. If I had to meet someone for the first time I would stutter, sweat and be inside my head trying to work out how to get away. The labels of fighter and leader I grasped with both hands because it helped me fake my way into feeling confident.

All this fighting, all this crime, all this drama . . . there was a deep method to our franticness.

I'm not sure if Stintz was aware – I don't suppose I was back then either – but each of these things we were up to was again the result of us searching to relax our thoughts a bit. At the time of us committing these devastating acts our thoughts were gone.

'You've got this, Punchy,' one of the boys barked at me from behind as I readied myself for a fight one Sunday afternoon. A park was the setting for our fight, the same park I used to kick the football around with my dad. Now years later I was hopefully going to stand above my knocked-out opponent. Bouncing from foot to foot as I warmed myself up, I looked over at the guy I was about to fight: he had a few boys in his corner and I had the same.

My thoughts teasing . . . *What if he has a weapon? Will he beat me? He's pretty big. So? Fuck him.*
Imagine what the boys will think if I lose . . . You won't lose.
You might.
I feel sick.
Let's get him.

Whack! My first punch brought silence – to my mind, that is. Fighting was an active meditation: no thoughts; stillness of mind. It was pleasurable. I look at everything that most people are addicted to or enjoy and it soon becomes evident that the addiction or joy is caused by a lust of stillness, of silence.

Take playing a sport, for example. You're totally present. A golfer isn't addicted to walking a course in shitty suit pants, nor do they enjoy hitting more bad shots than good. They're in love with those microseconds of pure bliss as their eyes scan that ball floating through the air. The world could be ending outside that golf course but none of that matters to a still mind.

Stintz was really a good kid, but he was still a kid. Other people his age were being influenced by sports stars or celebrities. His mentors, like me, were leading him to gaol.

'Well, fuck this,' I said a little louder to my zombie-like friends, trying to force some energy into myself and them. 'If we've got none left, let's go get some!'

So there we sat: Stintz and me. In a stolen car outside a unit block that housed a drug dealer.

It was a beautiful beachside suburb, morning walkers strutting past, their smiling faces, healthy figures and joyous energy seeming to glide them across the footpath. The setting summed up my contrasting existence – a microcosm of my entire life. Like my life, the outside environment didn't reflect what was happening on the inside. Soon a drug raid.

Fuck. What if he has a gun? Hope he has heaps of cash too. How many people are in there? Should've brought more boys with us, but then we'd have to split the cash up more. Maybe we will go back and get some more boys. Fuck doing it. I want to just go back to the house. I don't want to do this. What will the boys think if you bitch it? You have to go in.

Anyone watching us? Should I do this? Fuck, what will Dad do if I get busted? Arrgghhh!

'Alright, let's go.'

Silence . . .

The loud thoughts were gone. The blurry static washed away, and what was left was clean and pristine, a sense of ultimate presence. All my senses rose along with the hairs on my neck, but again the blissful still mind was there. This was what I desired.

As we soldiered across a grass patch still soaked with morning mist I zeroed in on the front security door. It was more a hindrance door than a security door for my fat foot with 120 kilos behind it.

My armed robbery meditation was underway.

My body was tense, every vein rushing with blood, my accomplice ferocious in his skipping step. The grass sped past my feet. But . . . my mind was still. Taking a presence-filled deep breath as though I was deep into a meditation, I leaned on my left leg and lifted my right foot.

BANG!

The hindrance door wasn't even that. It ripped off the hinges and fell inward like the first in line of standing dominos. It was loud. That sound meant disorder.

Stintz was right behind me as we bounced over the floored door and ran up carpeted steps. I could smell bacon cooking. Although the sounds of our raid were evident – doors smashing to the ground, our feet stomping upstairs – behind all of that was a stillness, a deep silence within my own mind. A focus. My thoughts were gone. It's what I always yearned for. It's what all of us want.

We had bought drugs off this guy before and knew exactly where his unit was. Two levels up sat our target. When we reached level one I heard a door slam closed. I noticed another open an inch, probably someone eyeing to see who had just trampled through their front security door. We didn't care about their restful Sunday morning; we only cared about the reprieve from our minds. We ran up the remaining staircase as I readied myself to kick down another door.

I froze. There he stood – our silent mind dealer. Standing outside his unit door barefooted, looking like he just woke up. He had no shirt on his white, skinny body. A faded, poorly designed dragon tattoo went from his belly button up over his chest. His hands were behind his back.

'Punchy!' I felt Stintz grab my right arm. 'Look out, he's got something.'

Our target heard what Stintz said and responded: 'It's only what you're after. I don't want any bullshit.' He revealed what he held in his hands: a plastic bag filled with smaller, sealed-up satchels.

Inside the satchels sat our little colourful pills of hope. Pills of solace. I went to smile before realising that wasn't what tough guys do.

'Where's the cash?' Stintz shot out.

'Come on, boys, I've got family here,' he pleaded.

'Well, you better want to go grab that cash then before we bust down that door too,' I said, nodding towards the blue front door that stood tall behind him.

'Wait a sec,' he said, handing me the bag of pills and turning around.

'Hey,' I said, grabbing his arm firmly. He turned and looked me in my eyes. 'Don't fuck around,' I growled.

He shook his head, and with a turn of a key opened his door before sliding inside, not wanting to reveal to those in the unit that he was being robbed.

'Bro,' Stintz said. I looked over at him, and although he was standing in the one spot he was bouncing a little. He was excited. He looked like a kid about to run out to a filled-up Christmas tree on 25 December. 'Let's just run in there!' he suggested.

'Nah, lad, just chill,' I said, looking around at the rest of the units. I could hear people moving around and I pictured them all looking through their peepholes at the robbery going on.

'Just chill,' I said again.

I heard the unclick of a lock on our target's blue door. He slid back out with another plastic bag, this time smaller.

'Here, it's all I've got. I'm done with this shit.' He passed the now-unwanted baton. It felt as though he was handing me his old life, ridding himself of the drama that being a drug dealer comes with. Drama I was happy to take for now.

'Look what we got, boys!' I said, entering the room filled with depleted bodies.

I threw the bag of pills on the ground and noticed a touch of energy rise in each person. Stintz sat on the floor to lie down. His energy went the other way.

A robbery can take it out of you.

'Open your mouth, brother,' I said to Stintz as I started throwing ecstasy at him. After four attempts one landed in his mouth and he chased it with some water.

'Throw me another,' he said, as I swallowed two.

These mornings were far too common. At the time I didn't know why I searched to always further my high. Often when off our faces on drugs I would get an insight into my boys' internal struggles.

'Punchy, I'm not looking forward to tomorrow when I'm coming down. I'm already doing my head in. I'm going to try to get a girl over to keep me company. I hate being by myself. You know what I mean?'

Before hearing things like this I thought I was the only one with the loud mind. I had no idea my boys were the same. We all suffered internally, so why did we keep doing things that ended in us suffering even more? At the time I didn't know why.

I do now.

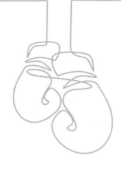

Chapter 2

A NEEDED DISCIPLINE

Life was finally beginning to look positive. During the last eight years I had committed crimes and hurt countless numbers of people, including myself.

With the scars of my past battles emblazoned across my head as a firm reminder of a life I once lived, I was attempting to let go of that heavy existence. Drugs, crime, street fights, graffiti and alcohol all combined to give me the image of a thug. A thug with power. I attached labels to myself that kept my true, pure self imprisoned. Standing guard to blockade any access to my soul was my near-impenetrable ego, wearing the armour of a harsh belief system imposed on me by my environment.

I had been stabbed twice, suffering a punctured lung during one of those stabbings, and was close to death on numerous other occasions. Having once been at the head of Sydney's most renowned street-fighting and graffiti crew meant I had witnessed horrible things that formed my view of the world as a place of violence. A week wouldn't pass without my knuckles slamming into the chin of another man.

I was surrounded by noise. Loud, shrieking noise.

Sounds of fights: fists on faces, feet stomping on heads, screams of pain, hollers of victory.

'Brother, fuck him up! You've got this, Punchy, knock him out!'

Sounds of relationship trouble: arguing, crying, blaming, swearing, defending, sex, fights over no sex, breaking up and making up.

'I hate you. I can't believe you would do this again. Who is she? You told me you loved me. I hate you!'

Sounds of graffiti: track rocks crunching, spray cans spraying, trains careening past, fences being cut and alarms going off.

'Security is coming. Hurry up, let's go! They're right there. Run!'

Sounds of death: friends hit by trains, friends dropping from drugs, news reports of friends killing someone, my father sobbing as he held my lifeless grandma.

'You're not going to die, my man! Hold on, keep your eyes open. Open your eyes!'

And the loudest of all, the *sounds of my mind*, echoing constantly.

Endless . . .

Don't do that. What will people think if you don't do it? Who cares! What do you mean, who cares? You're supposed to be the main man.

I hope I don't get caught. No way you will. Yes, you will, you messed up.

I hope she likes me. You're fat, no way she will. Yeah, but you've got a bad boy reputation, girls love that. She won't.

What's that guy looking at? Hit him. Nah, don't, there's innocent people around. Fuck them; just do it.

What will Mum and Dad think? I can't let them down. Yeah, but you can't back down.

What will everyone think?

I should get a job. Why? You hate working. Imagine everything you will miss out on. You don't need that much money anyways.

I need some drugs. I think we should have a break. I want drugs! Where can I get them? Do the boys have any? I need to get some money!

He made you look bad. Why is he talking shit? Fuck him up. You gotta get him! Let it go; who cares. What will the boys think? You have to get him. You can't do that, you might kill him. You have to!

And the thoughts went on . . . and on.

To better my life I knew what I needed: silence.

Life was manic and I was the cause. My mind was stuck on fear, anxiety and attack and forever defending my image, an image that was only real in my mind. By putting that energy out into the world it wasn't long before I was down a deep dark hole, and each day I dug a little deeper.

I had always known right from wrong but would rarely listen to my feelings. Instead, I'd have an internal battle of my mind telling me what to do or my heart feeling what was ultimate truth. My mind with its conditioned worries and defences would win the majority of the time, and then after listening to the worries of my mind and usually hurting people in the process my thoughts would be even louder as I was flooded with more guilt and worries – a vicious and scary cycle.

It was time for change.

After years of being a street fighter I had some dark, depressing nights filled with tears and fear. Tears of regret. Tears of witnessing friends dying. Tears as I tried to escape my mind. Fear. Fear of retribution after I attacked somebody who had a large crew backing them. Fear of police running through my house to take me to gaol. Fear . . . immense fear of my noisy thoughts.

I didn't want that any more. Visually, too, I was a mess. Weighing in at over 120 kilos, I knew I had to lose the weight to lose the attitude.

There were endless things that could have made me snap out of the crazy life. I mean, I had been stabbed twice and almost killed. Nope, didn't stop me. It actually was just another event that boosted my mind-made image. Now I had been stabbed and had survived.

Watching a friend drop dead in front of me on drugs – nah, didn't stop my drug abuse.

Pulling my friend off the train tracks after he had been run over by a train, severing his arm – I kept painting trains. That didn't affect me.

Endless friends crushing their own and their families' lives by being sent to gaol for doing things that weren't as bad as what I was getting up to. *They won't catch me. Besides, if they do I'll see a heap of my boys inside gaol.* That threat didn't stop me.

Sure, all this stuff worried me and made my thoughts smash me with regret and fear, but it wasn't going to make me turn it all around.

No outside circumstance was strong or scary enough to take over my destructive ego. It doesn't matter what people said to me, who wanted to help me, how many guys stomped their feet on my head or how many years my boys faced in gaol: all this stuff was just life back then and was a part of my identity. Without this drama who was I? Now, that thought was scary.

The change starts within. Sure, people can plant seeds of hope and inspiration but you can't change people. The only thing that can be done for others is to be an example.

Lead, shine and hope they come on the journey with you. To help you can just plant those seeds and set a good example. None of us are perfect, but if you stay true to yourself and don't let others bring you down then those you want to help will be inspired to better their lives. If not, that's their path.

So how did I start?

There was some infighting within our crew. I had been stabbed in the head with two broken bottles, resulting in more than 100 staples in my head and the top of my right ear having to be surgically reattached. That was one of my boys . . . He almost killed me. A part of the team I had shed blood for over many years, and he tried to kill me.

From that moment the crew was never the same. There was a split in the crew that resulted in new crews being formed. I wanted it to all go away. I was over the paranoia, the ego-driven actions, the hate-filled thoughts. I just didn't know what to do.

I lived with my parents, and my home was visited by two detectives one afternoon. I missed them but they left their details. Mum didn't tell Dad they had been, so to avoid another possible visit that would result in Dad losing his shit I called the detectives, who asked me to meet them in the city.

I grew up with it deeply embedded in me that you don't speak to police. I thought being on the front foot was a better option here, though, because if I just avoided them the paranoia about what they wanted and constant worry of them knocking on my door while Dad was home would have eaten away at me. I met with them to see what they wanted, and the worries before the meeting were compounded afterwards when I found out they knew more about me and my crew than I thought possible. They called me by my nickname and wanted me to tell them who it was who had stabbed me, and continued to push with questions.

I sat there stunned with what they knew about me.

'I'm out of all the drama. I just want to be left alone.'

I was hoping it would give me the breathing space to start making some choices that would turn my life around.

A few months after that meeting I was convinced by a few of the boys to head down to Melbourne to paint trains. Our crew was composed of fighters and graffiti artists, so painting trains was another thing I loved – the painting brought the stillness.

We ended up getting caught by police while painting trains in Melbourne and being charged with numerous offences. A few weeks later I was at work back in Sydney when I received a message on my phone. It was my brother telling me to call his phone, not the house phone.

I knew why.

'Bro, there's fucking coppers here raiding the house.'

Normal people would have been worried, but for me I saw it as a reason to justify my change. After getting my family home raided by the police, it was a bit of a relief for me. I used the possibility of serving gaol time as a reason to pull back from the crew. It would rest my body but, more crucially for me, it would hopefully relax my thoughts a little.

I had a girlfriend, Anne, who I met when I was 17 and she was 16. When I met her she was seeing one of the boys in my crew. Impressed with my higher status in the gang and, I like to think, my good looks, she showed an interest in me. Soon we were dating and she was staying with me at my parents' place, where I lived in the granny flat out back.

When I met Anne she was a soft young girl who came from a nice upbringing. You are your environment, though, and soon her mouth was up there with the harshness of my words. We had a volatile relationship in which fights were more common than romance. She had my back, though, and I had hers.

'Love you, baby. I will do anything for you,' she used to say in her sweet, innocent tone; then a moment later after I was being suss on my phone with another girl: 'Who the fuck you speaking to? If I fucking find out you're messing around I'll crush you and that other bitch.'

We both had a lot of internal battles, reactive patterns and emotions we had no idea how to understand, feel or process. As young adults who didn't know what we were doing, the fights, make ups and break ups seemed to be just part of what a relationship was. We reactively expelled all of our own stuff onto each other, which left us both confused and angry. I needed to be alone to figure out who I was, and so did she, but we ended up with each other and drowning in a triggered, toxic and emotional cocktail . . . with moments of what we thought were love.

It was good to have Anne around to help with my worries about my impending court date; I leant on her as more of a distraction from my internal battles than as a lover. When I was feeling good I was nowhere to be seen, but after a drug binge that left me feeling dark I needed her company to hug away my loud mind.

'Mr Kennedy, I'm considering a custodial sentence.' The judge spewed over me with his words. He looked younger than I thought he would be, had slick black hair and spoke with ultimate confidence, knowing his words had power – the power to put a halt to a young man's freedom.

Before that moment I'd thought I was going home. Sure, I'd boasted to the boys that I might get locked up, but I didn't think it would really happen.

I felt weak. My body swayed a little and my nerves felt as though they were eating at my skin. I tried to maintain my composure in front of one of my friends but my fake smile wasn't lessening the tension in my body. I was worried. I was hot. I could be going to gaol.

Regardless of what's happening in the outside world, how tough someone looks or what demographic they're from – age, sex, religion, race: it doesn't matter – we all suffer the same internal battles: worrying what people think, having to live up to labels and expectations, social awkwardness, anxiety, coping with past trauma and not knowing who we really are or where to fit in. However, some people manage it better while others are magicians at hiding it.

I don't know if I was hiding my internal battles here, though.

When I walked back into court my legs were a bit shaky as I lowered myself into my seat at the front of the court.

'Mr Kennedy, stand.' I stood back up. My feet were unsteady and my world was rocking from side to side.

'You and your co-accused organised a carload of men to come to our state to wreak havoc on our train system. You are a criminal gang who are a burden to this society. You should be locked away.'

I tried to look remorseful. I nodded my head, hoping that by agreeing with the judge it would help my cause. I thought I was going to faint and was close to falling into my chair.

The judge licked his finger and picked up some papers, looking at the photos of the trains we had painted. 'Grown men painting on a train? It doesn't even *look* good.'

Why don't you lay the boot in while I'm down, I thought. I felt like an idiot. I wanted to interrupt him to explain the culture of painting and that there was a lot more to it than just vandalism. I imagined people behind me rolling their eyes and thinking we were just immature men painting on a train, and now we would be locked up for it.

Then, with seven words, the judge saved my life: 'I will give you your last chance.'

I was given an 18-month good behaviour bond and fined $5,000.

Walking out of the court alone, I looked up at the sunny sky and felt weightless. I pulled my phone out of my pocket and saw that I had 16 missed calls from home. It made me smile.

'This is it,' I whispered to myself. Time for complete change.

Returning to Sydney, I upped my training and turned it into an obsession. I would wake at 4.30 am to do running sprints at the park, and then in the evening do weights in my garage. I started seeing faster results: I lost 10 kilos, then I trained harder and got to a 20-kilo loss before I asked Dad to start training me.

'Dad, remember how I asked you to teach me to fight? Well, can you teach me how to box?'

'Yeah, I'd love to. I just need you to stay focused and lose more weight.' He was testing me to see if I really wanted it.

I ended my relationship with Anne. I still loved her, but what we had together wasn't working and it was the best outcome for both of us. It wasn't the cleanest break-up, though, and after hours of heated arguments I removed all of my stuff from her place.

For the first time as an adult I was single. I wanted to focus on myself and have no one to answer to. It was time to work on me.

Six malice-free months went past, and my drug and alcohol intake had reduced so much it was almost completely out of my life.

I noticed my parents smiling more; they didn't have to worry about me so much. In the past they had visited me in hospitals or police stations after another crew had smashed me with retribution or because I'd broken the law.

Dad was helping me in the garage by holding the boxing pads. 'Luke, I love training you but you need to get to a fighter's gym. You've gotta get around other fighters.'

I was nervous at the thought. I pictured a bunch of warriors skipping rope in unison, boxing bags getting demolished behind them as fighters sparred in the ring. The idea of that was a menacing thought to someone who was a novice boxer. I could fight in the street, but that was totally different to the skills required of a boxer. Boxers were like gods to me, and the idea of setting foot into their training ground made me anxious.

'Go train with your brother, he's at a good gym,' Dad said as we finished up our session.

Ruben, who was three years older than me, was training for an upcoming fight. He was a professional and had been fighting for almost 10 years. I loved going to watch him fight: he was short and thin and really quick in the ring. He could avoid punches easily and counter with his own.

'Bro, I'm coming to train with you soon,' I said to Ruben.

'Sweet, come tomorrow.' He laughed as though I didn't know what I was in for.

The next day Ruben drove me to the gym; I was incredibly nervous as we pulled up out the front. When I grabbed my bag from the boot I heard someone say: 'Hey, Ruben, how you doing, champ?' I looked up to see a short, chubby man walking towards Ruben.

'Stan, this is my brother Luke,' Ruben introduced us.

Stan shook my hand. 'So, you want to fight?' he asked, still holding on to my hand.

'Sure do,' I smiled.

He looked me in the eyes. 'Well, let's go,' he said, gesturing towards an open door.

As I was walking up the stairs of the warehouse that the gym was on top of I could smell sweat. When I reached the top of the stairs I looked around the large space. The walls were lined with full-length mirrors and posters of old fighters, while boxing bags hung from gaps in the ceiling. A small boxing ring stood at the back of the room that I was itching to jump into.

I like this!

I ended up losing nearly 50 kilos and then my first fight was organised.

'Luke, me and your mum are so proud of you,' Dad said a couple of nights before the fight. 'You've shown discipline I didn't know you had.'

I liked the idea of discipline: it was something a warrior would have. I wanted to increase this discipline and promised myself I would never again throw another punch outside the ring.

On the night of my first fight, as I sat in the dressing room, a constant stream of people came in to wish me luck.

Dad was shepherding his friends in to meet me. 'This is my boy. He's having his first fight tonight.' I could tell how happy he was to introduce me as his son.

'Mate, just work on your jab,' Dad advised. 'You've got a good jab – keep using it. We're all proud of you, even your brother. Ruben, go on: tell your brother how proud you are,' Dad said.

Ruben laughed. 'Alright, I'm proud of you,' he squeezed out.

The stage was set for the beginning of a new life. The ring of the bell for the first round would signal my complete turnaround.

As I walked out to the ring I heard cheers from voices I recognised as my boys. I could practically smell the beer on the breath of the people cheering in their seats.

'Here we go, Punchy!' someone hollered, slapping me on my back. They were all there to support me as always.

My body shook a little with anticipation, but a huge smile spread the width of my face. I jumped through the ropes into the ring and looked down at my feet as they bounced a little on the soft white canvas, which was stained with spots of blood. Outside the ring the crowd sat in darkness. I looked across at my opponent, dressed in blue. He was shorter than me but broader.

He looked strong. His trainer was speaking to him out of the side of his mouth as he stared at me.

'Fuck him up, Punchy!' Voices from the darkness cheered for blood.

Fuck, this is incredible! I wonder how I look. How many of these people are here for me? Does this guy look like he will beat me? You can't tell. I wonder how hard he trained. Not as hard as me. You did miss that session last week. I wonder if he missed a session. If he didn't he's probably fitter.

Ding!

The bell rang for the first round, and the thoughts were gone.

I came out the only way I knew how: throwing a heap of punches. He was doing the same, and I got caught with a massive hit. I heard the crowd moan as the thud of his landed punch echoed off the walls in the small arena.

That made me mad.

You're getting beat in front of the boys! What are they thinking? Dad thinks I can't fight.

Fuck!

Now my head wasn't in the fight. Instead, I was watching it through the eyes of the crowd.

I went on to get it over him. The ref stopped my onslaught in the first round after some scrappy punching resulted in my opponent being cradled in a corner.

I'd won!

I screamed and high-fived Stan, my short, round-headed trainer. He looked just as happy as I was. I wasn't screaming in delight about the win so much as my triumph over eight years of fighting, crime, drugs, drama, alcohol and stabbings and a relentless mind that wouldn't let me be. When the referee stood between my opponent and me waving his arms for the fight to stop, it was as though he was also waving away the old me. My past was gone; my new life was about to begin.

I walked over to Dad and he congratulated me. 'Mate, you did well, but you've got to work on throwing that jab properly.' As soon as he said it I knew I hadn't looked good. 'I'm proud of you for getting in there, but we just need to work on a few things.'

He was right: I was a complete novice.

'Punchy, brother!' Stintz hugged me, a flurry of excited shouts. 'Man, how was it? No one can stop you. I want to jump in that ring too! You reckon I could?' He was always excited.

A couple of years later I trained Stintz for his first fight.

It was a battle getting him to training because there were weeks he would disappear on a drug binge or robbing spree. I had to chase him around Sydney and pick him up from different places just to get him to training. He had his doubts, and suffered with some dark demons. I knew he would be a great boxer.

The day of his fight he was extremely nervous and excited. He didn't train much in the week leading up to it, and his face told me he had had a couple of drug-fuelled nights. He fought his heart out and was the easy winner. He won fighter of the night and received a huge trophy. Hugging me after the fight, he said: 'Punchy, this is the best moment of my life. All my family are here and it's the first time I've really made them proud. I'm proud of myself. I love you, Punchy. Thank you for doing this for me!'

'Brother, this is just the beginning. You did this without even training much. You're going to be something special.'

Not long after his house was raided and he was back behind bars.

I won my first three fights by knockout and was on top of the world. I started helping out people at the gym, young kids who needed some guidance, rather than hurting people in the streets, and I knew this was the life I wanted. It felt good.

There was another reason I was happy: my relationship with Ruben was getting stronger. We had rarely hung out since high school. When we were young I looked up to him but he wouldn't have much to do with me, frequently shooing me away. Growing up it was much the same: he had his friends, I had mine. We wouldn't chat about anything. If I asked how he was he would simply respond with 'Good', like a kid responding to a parent about a day at school. Training brought us a little closer together, and we started to appreciate the time with each other more.

I was proud of myself. I wanted to do even better.

I wanted a career that me and my parents would be proud of. I wanted something that would make me feel strong, a career that was different. I wasn't good with making things or handyman stuff, nor was I looking to do a trade. I wanted to be like a warrior.

I decided the navy was my calling.

The first time I told Mum that I was joining I saw tears in her eyes. She was incredibly proud.

After completing the knowledge test I was offered numerous roles that matched my results. I researched the position of boatswain's mate and decided that's what I wanted. I was confident and the happiest I had been in my whole life. I was three months out from my final physical, which I would have passed easily, and I had a buzzing energy about me. One afternoon I was training at the gym and was approached by Stan, who had just gotten off the phone after speaking with a fight promoter. He told me I had a fight coming up in eight weeks' time.

Even though I responded with a loud 'Fuck, yeah!', butterflies raged in my stomach. As I stared at my reflection in the gym's mirror while skipping rope my mind reeled. With each skip of the rope, each slap against the gym's floor, a new thought came crashing through.

You're going to get knocked out!

Skip.

Everybody is going to laugh at you.

Skip.

You haven't trained hard enough, he will be fitter.

Skip.

What if you don't make weight and the fight has to be called off on the night?

A wake of wind was blowing against the top of my head as the skipping rope came within millimetres, and I bounced from foot to foot as the white rope tapped the floor and glided under my gold-trimmed black boxing shoes.

You're going to get beat!

My loud mind barked endlessly.

Whip! The rope snapping me in the back of the head pulled me out of my negative trance and quieted my mind. The pain of the rope was a welcome distraction, its burning sensation the catalyst for focus and dulling the rattling in my head.

Although life was changing I was still dominated by a berserk mind. My mind would look for the worst in any situation then, to try to feel better, I would work my way backwards to get closer to reality.

You have been training hard, you will win this easily.

After a heavy training session I would head home on my motorbike. While cruising down the road and wiping the fog clear of my helmet visor, I would smile. Riding my bike gave me a sense of freedom. The wind tickling my face and sneaking in through the spaces of my helmet would make the endorphins flow, and for that short time my mind would rest long enough for me to be at peace.

At home that night, pondering yet another hard couple of months training before the next fight, I sat down to watch the six o'clock news. As a young child I would sit with my dad to watch the news. I'd listen intently to his comments on each story and notice him switch moods from story to story, laughing one minute and shaking his head and swearing the next. The news was, and is, like that: it more often than not dishes out bad news with a mix of something humorous in there to keep you glued to it.

I heard my phone ring. I answered it and heard Ruben's voice before I could speak. 'Hey, I've booked a trip to Thailand on Thursday.'

'Again?' I replied. He had visited the country more times than I had travelled out of Sydney.

'Yeah, come with me,' he said.

'Nah, man, I can't,' I said, not sure he was serious and knowing he normally wouldn't invite me anywhere. I guess boxing really did bring us closer together.

'Seriously, come. You're joining the navy at the start of next year and fighting in eight weeks. This can be your last hurrah.' It seemed he had this script ready.

'No way: it's in four days and I've got no money,' I said honestly. My mind filled with an array of excuses from a lack of funds to my fear of his short temper, which I could never understand growing up. What would travelling internationally with him be like?

'Get a loan.'

'I just got a loan for my bike!' The bike I rode home was only a couple of months old.

'See if the bank will increase it,' he shot back.

'I'm fighting in eight weeks.'

'Eight weeks is plenty of time to prepare for a fight,' he said, as if I was being stupid.

'I've got to work.'

'Ask for time off,' he begged.

'Impossible!'

'Just ask.'

Like the boxer he was, Ruben countered everything I threw at him. I hung up the phone and sat watching the news but I couldn't get his voice out of my mind. *Eight weeks is plenty of time to prepare for a fight. You are joining the navy soon, this could be your last hurrah.*

I was trying to convince myself to go.

I had been to Thailand a few years earlier with Anne and had enjoyed myself. Going with Ruben would be a completely different trip.

I called Ruben back. 'Okay. If work lets me have the time off and if the bank gives me a loan then surely it's meant to be.'

'*Yes!*' Ruben was ecstatic.

'I'll give it a go,' I said, still not believing any of it was possible. The past was the past. Boxing had helped Ruben and I connect and this trip would deepen that connection.

After hanging up the phone I sat contemplating the conversation I was about to have with my boss. I hated making phone calls to people I didn't really know, especially to an authority figure. Always up inside my head my mind would tease and I'd convince myself that these authority figures thought wrongly of me.

Just relax and don't stutter. He's just a man. Who cares what he thinks? What if I sound stupid? I'll tell him Ruben bought me a ticket as a surprise. He's going to know you're talking shit. No way will they believe Ruben bought me a ticket. What if I get fired? The belting noise would scream away.

Before going into any conversation I would predetermine the responses and thoughts, so depending on what I thought they would think I would lie to try to control how I was perceived. After turning my life around, in the beginning I would attempt to control everyone's opinion of me and hope they liked me. It's even a battle now from time to time. I'd leave every conversation stuck in my head, replaying what had just happened and hoping certain words weren't taken the wrong way. Any interaction I'd have with people felt like an arm wrestle . . . with myself.

'Hi, mate, my brother just called me and gave me a ticket to Thailand as an early Christmas present.'

'Wow! What a great brother.'

Shit, he's on to me! That sounded sarcastic!

'Yeah, I know, I couldn't believe it! Problem is the flight leaves this Thursday.'

'*This* Thursday?' he spat back.

'Yeah, I know it's soon, it's cool if you guys say no. I'll just tell him I can't go.'

I tried not to smile to myself as tension filled my chest. I knew full well he wouldn't deny me my early Christmas present, especially if it was already paid for.

No way will they say no to my brother giving me a Christmas present. This will work!

'No, you can't do that. We will get you covered,' he said, a little disappointed.

Yes!

'Really? Thanks so much, mate.'

One down; one to go. Surely the bank wouldn't let me increase my loan?

What if I can't get the loan? What will I say to my boss?

The next day I walked into the bank and straight into the office of the lovely lady who helped me get the first loan for my bike.

'Good to see you again, Luke.' She gestured for me to sit down. 'How's the bike?'

'The bike is going great! I love it. So much freedom.'

'Good to hear. So what brings you back?'

'Umm . . . I'm going to propose to my girlfriend in Thailand. I need some money for the trip and an engagement ring. Can I get a loan on top of my current loan?'

'Shouldn't be an issue. How much do you need?'

'Worked it all out, and I need about eight thousand.' I needed to get $8,000 because Ruben had asked me if he could borrow some cash off me if the loan was approved. Is that why he wanted me to go?

I walked out of there $8,000 richer. Two from two seemingly impossible outcomes. Getting the loan authorised and scoring the time off work had been a long shot, yet here I was. This trip was definitely meant to be! Everything had fallen into place.

I was a little confused and still not sure I wanted to go, but now I had to.

Thailand was my destiny.

I called Ruben to give him the good news.

'I'm coming.'

That night I was warming up on the skipping rope for the thousandth time when I broke the news to Stan.

'I'm going to Thailand on Thursday with Ruben.'

The snap of the rope on the floor accentuated the look on Stan's face: he was worried. 'What about the fight?'

'Mate, everything will be alright.' I tried to calm him.

'Please be careful, Punchy. You can't fuck up and carry on over there like you do here. No drugs, mate, you can't do drugs there!'

He knew I could go and still have more than enough time to prepare for the fight, but I could tell he thought this trip spelt trouble. He had only known me for about six months, but in that time he had learned of my dangerous partying ways.

'Stan, I'm not that dumb.' Knowing Thailand's harsh stance against drugs, there was no way I was messing with that shit.

The night before the trip I stayed with my parents. In the morning, Dad sat down next to me as I was putting on my shoes.

'Luke, me and your mum are worried about this trip,' he said as Mum entered the room to listen in.

'Please, us Kennedy boys can't handle the drink. Stay off it, mate, it's all a big lie. Everyone thinks you have to drink to have a good time. It's bullshit. Alcohol killed my mother. Kennedys are not meant to drink.'

He was right: whenever one of the Kennedy family had a drink there was almost always some drama. Dad had found Jesus, and he had quit drinking a year earlier and was trying desperately to make all of his children do the same.

'You're my boy. Please just be careful. You can have fun without alcohol.'

He gave me pretty much the same lecture Stan had, without the mention of drugs. My parents were always concerned about us kids, and this trip increased their anxiety. But for me it was less about the alcohol and more about the drugs, and they didn't know that and they certainly didn't have to.

'We love you, mate,' Dad said before kissing me on the forehead and leaving the room. Mum smiled at me and sat down and gave me a long hug and a kiss. 'Love you, Luke,' she said before following Dad outside. I went to my room to pack.

'Bro, why you bringing that?' Ruben asked as he noticed me packing a mouth guard into my suitcase.

'I want to do some training over there and might be able to spar with someone,' I replied, a little embarrassed at him questioning me.

'Man, we won't be doing any training on this trip,' he laughed, placing a handful of condoms into his bag before picking up a box.

'Look what I got,' he said as I was zipping up my full suitcase. The box he held contained a new camera.

'Nice!'

'I got it yesterday. Cost me twelve hundred so we have to look after it.'

Ruben enjoyed travelling, but what he loved more was showing people photos of the adventures on his trips. Buying an expensive camera would increase this love.

He zipped his bag up; it was almost empty. 'Where's all your stuff?' I asked.

'I'm buying new clothes over there.'

'With the money I gave you?' I smirked.

'Yep,' he giggled. 'Clothes are cheap there anyways.'

'Let's go, there might be traffic,' Dad called out from the lounge room.

I looked at Ruben and he nodded his head. 'Let's go,' he said softly.

'Let's.'

I walked into the lounge room and saw Mum standing near the front door. 'Love you, Mum,' I said as I kissed her forehead.

'Love you too, Luke.' She smiled a nervous smile.

I was incredibly excited as we made our way to the car. Dad walked ahead as Ruben whispered into my ear so Dad couldn't hear: 'You ready for the trip of a lifetime? Let's party!'

Dad looked back and saw Ruben whispering. He shook his head and jumped into the car.

'Chill, bro,' I whispered back to Ruben. I didn't want to give Dad a reason to worry.

I jumped in the front passenger seat. Dad started speaking but I was up in my loud mind.

Trip of a lifetime. He thinks he can party? Wait until I show him how it's done. Man, I'm going to cut loose on this trip.

Don't mess up too much. Let's have fun but don't be crazy. Fuck it, let's enjoy ourselves.

'Boys, please.' Dad grabbed my leg, knowing I wasn't listening. 'Me and your mum are worried about you. Have a good time but just be careful. It would crush me if anything went wrong.' He looked concerned.

'Relax, Dad. Ruben has been there heaps, we'll be sweet.' I attempted to lessen his worries.

Although Ruben and I never went out and hit the town with each other, I was looking forward to partying with him on this holiday and enjoying our first real outing together.

I stared out the window as the Sydney streets flew by, old factories and newly developed unit blocks sitting side by side with shops and offices at the bottom. The city skyline was in the background, Centrepoint Tower providing a dead giveaway that it was Sydney.

'Ahhh, fuck this!' Dad moaned as we stopped in Sydney's infamous traffic. He hated traffic.

I could feel Dad's tense energy as I stared out the window so I looked over to see what he was up to. His head was going from side to side as he glanced at both side mirrors, then he gave a quick snap of his head to look behind. He was looking for a gap in the slow traffic to advance a little further in the queue.

'Knew we should've fucking left earlier!' he said sternly.

'We've got heaps of time, Dad, just chill.' I turned and looked back out the window.

A homeless man was begging for money as a man in a suit walked by on his phone, not even noticing.

'It could be worse, we could be that guy,' I said to Dad, gesturing with my head over to the homeless man.

Dad let out a big sigh and put his hand on my leg. 'You're right. I'm with my boys, I'm blessed. I've just gotta chill. Sorry, boys.'

When up in his head and anxious he could be very snappy and lack even a slight taste of empathy. When brought back to the present moment with a prime example that there's nothing to really be angry about he could be incredibly soft and apologetic.

'Again, I'm sorry, I didn't mean to get angry.'

Why is Dad so worried? Hope he's not going to jinx this trip. You don't believe in that shit. Just relax. All will be sweet!

We got to the airport around lunchtime to begin the trip of a lifetime. We hopped out of the car and kissed Dad goodbye.

'Love you both,' he called out as we closed the car door, his words muffled by the sounds of a busy airport: the engines of cars, vans and mini buses revving, tyres screeching, ushers blowing whistles and security guards barking orders.

'Get out of way!' a taxi driver yelled in broken English as he beeped his horn. All this franticness as drivers looked for spots to drop off their passengers.

We made our entrance through the airport doors, the busy drop-off course left behind, but what remained was a traffic of people – families, backpackers and businesspeople, all with one objective: get my arse on a plane.

Hope the trip is going to be good. Ruben will show me heaps. It's going to be fun. Can't wait to get drunk. Fuck, did I leave anything at home? Shouldn't have brought my mouthguard. Yeah, you should have, we will train over there.

You're not going to train.

Yeah, I will.

See what happens.

*Wonder how long the flight is? Can't wait for a drink. Think
I need to go to the toilet. Nah, I can hold it. Probably not. Where is
the toilet? Fuck it, just hold it until we book in.*

I looked down at Ruben – he was nearly a foot shorter than
me – and smiled. He didn't return the smile, instead pushing
me awkwardly. Ruben hardly ever showed his emotions,
preferring to tell me to 'Get fucked' than say anything nice.
Did this hide how he felt, throwing up a block to who he
really was? Occasionally I would watch him laugh and drop his
guard, knowing he was being himself, and it warmed my heart.
I wondered what his mind was saying to him.

'This is going to be the best,' I laughed.

We waited in line to put our baggage through, and I was
itching for a drink. I'd been concentrating on my training and
upcoming fight so I hadn't had a decent drink in more than four
months. I was ready for a big one. Once we got through security
we hustled our way over to the first airport bar we could find
so Ruben could tell me about the trip he had in store for us.
He liked to play tour guide.

'Bro, wait till you see these clubs! We are going to have
the best time. Last time I was here, I –' Ruben continued
talking about his past trips to Thailand but I drifted off into
my mind . . . again. His punching of the air brought me
back, though. 'All the women there are next level!' He was
animated in his description.

I felt good after a few drinks and rested my arms on top of the shiny wooden bar bench as I sat next to Ruben. The sharp-looking bar tender poured our drinks; there was nobody else in the bar.

'Let's go,' Ruben said as he sculled the remainder of his drink. We had some time for shopping before boarding our flight. Duty-free shopping.

'Man, look how cheap these nice watches are,' Ruben said.

I checked them out briefly and then kept walking. My right elbow clipped something and I heard glass tapping on glass. It was a shelf filled with big bottles of rum, my drink of choice. I grabbed them.

Ruben stopped me. 'Why are you grabbing that here? You can just order cheap drinks when we get there.'

'I want it now. What if they have no rum there?' I argued. I didn't want to risk a shortage of it.

He rolled his eyes. 'Bro, please don't start acting up.' Ruben knew that when I started to drink rum, especially if I had a full bottle, I would cause trouble.

'Relax,' I said, reaching to grab the bottles.

'Come on, no mucking up. We can get alcohol there!' he added.

I noticed the frustration and sensed nervousness about him.

'What? Loosen up, man!' Now I was a little frustrated.

Ruben enjoyed a good time, but he was more about fun and laughter while I could get reckless and stupid. *Did he still want me here?* I worried for a second. I shrugged it off and headed into the restrooms with a bottle of Coke. It splashed into the toilet bowl as I emptied half of the bottle's contents and filled it back up with rum. *This should do me while waiting for our flight.*

And just like that I was set.

As we queued to board our plane I glanced around at the line of people. I noticed a few tired faces. *They look miserable. Must be heading home from a holiday. I hate it when a holiday finishes too, but fucking lighten up.* I then saw some others who looked excited. *They must be starting theirs, they're pumped to go. How good is the feeling before a trip? I love this shit!*

Not only did I love people watching, but I also loved to judge every situation and make up a whole world of scenarios in my head. Who knows what these people were doing? My ego, my mind, always thought it knew best. I would judge somebody in a split second and make up my mind about them.

* * *

I got massages from a local masseuse who practised Chinese medicine. I visited him weekly, as it helped with my recovery from training so hard, and I always arrived five minutes early. One time there was an older man seated in the waiting room speaking with the masseuse about some herbs, and I took a seat next to him.

'Hi, son,' the older man greeted me with a smile before turning back to the masseuse.

'Hi,' I smiled.

This better not take too much longer; my massage is a few minutes away, I thought as they chatted.

'Take this in tea five time day,' the Chinese masseuse said in his broken English as he packed some herbs into a brown bag.

39

'Four times?' The older man leaned in closer to hear.

He said five times, I thought, shaking my head a little. My impatience was creeping up on me.

'Five time,' the masseuse responded.

'Okay, how much of the other stuff again?' the older man asked.

Fucking hell! I thought, and I sighed a little as I shuffled in my seat. I glanced at my phone and noticed it was now two minutes past the start time of my massage.

My impatience came from my dad. Like he was in the traffic, I thought being stuck and not moving or progressing slowly meant disaster. Even if there was nothing to rush for, even if I was going to be early but was still was going slowly I would get agitated. Having to wait, even for a chilled-out massage, resulted in tension. We are a product of our environment, and while growing up I would watch my dad be relaxed one moment then merge into an anxious wrecking ball the second he had to wait longer than he wanted to.

'I write it all down for you,' the masseuse smiled as he sat down at his desk. He pulled a drawer open and grabbed a notepad.

Every second felt like an hour.

The older man covered his mouth to cough.

Great, now I'll get sick. My impatience and tension would suffocate any positive possibility.

'Five times of this bag. One time this one,' the masseuse continued.

Are you serious? Hurry up! I felt my jaw clench a little and my head felt cloudy. My anxiety volcano was about to erupt, and the

Chinese man's patience was reducing mine even further. At five minutes past the time I was supposed to start I coughed a fake cough, hoping they would remember I was in the room.

'I hear this guy is the best,' the older man said to me, nodding his head towards the masseuse.

'Yeah, he gives a great massage,' I said, hoping to remind them what I was there for.

'Hope he can fix me; doc's given me three months,' he said casually.

'Huh?' I responded. It felt as though his words had smacked me in the face.

'Cancer.' He sat and folded his arms, and leant back further in his chair. 'Doctor said I'm lucky if I live another three months, that's why I'm here. I hear this guy can help.' He looked over at the masseuse, who gave a sympathetic smile.

'I'm sorry, mate,' I said, and I put my hand on his shoulder. Like my dad, when something dragged me out of my bullshit head and made me realise what a selfish prick I had been, all that was left was sympathy.

'I'll be okay. If not, I'm going to love every second of these three months,' he said as he stood up to grab his hope-filled brown bags.

I watched as he left the room, the door closing behind him signifying to me that it was the last time I'd ever see that man. My mind felt a little clearer, my body relaxed.

When I was out of my head there wasn't anything to be anxious about.

'Luke,' the masseuse said. 'Thank you for your patience. That poor man live not much longer. Come on, your turn.'

I just sat still.

'Luke, come on, your massage start. You don't want to run out of time sitting there.'

Sometimes I'd get smacked in the face with the truth and hate myself for being so judgemental.

* * *

I sculled some more of my mixed drink. 'I'm feeling pretty fucked,' I said loudly, and laughed along with Ruben. A lady standing next to me stared into my eyes and shook her head slowly after I swore and boisterously pushed Ruben. No doubt she could smell the rum.

From under her breath she said: 'Loser.'

Why did I say that? Why do I always do that stupid shit? I'm an idiot, I thought to myself. My dad always said, 'The smart ones go unheard, the smart ones shut their mouths.' Once I took a sip of alcohol I would end up in shit after forgetting his advice. I quickly sobered up as I imagined what I looked like from her eyes.

I did this regularly, caring what other people thought. It could be a good thing, like on this occasion, which made me realise I was acting like a loser. Most times, though, caring so much about what other people thought stopped me from living a real experience. Even while eating in a restaurant with my family I would worry that other people were annoyed at my family's loud laughter and conversation. I couldn't sit and enjoy the company. I would then get angry at myself for not living in the moment, which would take me even further away from it.

Worrying what other people think has always been a battle, and still is. I have lessened it, though.

On the plane, flying Thai Airways, I was loving life. Free alcohol! They were serving Hennessy for free. I loved Hennessy. In my thieving days I could rarely afford it so I would steal it, and now it was free!

'Bro, it's not funny any more. You can't get buckled on the plane. You can get in trouble.'

'I won't,' I slurred a little.

Going by Ruben's frown, clenched jaw and deep nasal breathing, his frustration had doubled and he started to get the shits with me.

After 15 minutes in the air I had already downed two drinks and was laughing loudly.

'Bro, settle down. Everyone is getting dirty on you. You're too loud,' he grunted, grabbing my arm. He pointed to people who were whispering to each other.

I simply laughed at their misfortune for having to listen to me. I was drunk then so I didn't care what other people thought.

Alcohol skewed my perception. It boosted my ego and made me obnoxious. I would interrupt people's conversations and refuse to be quiet. Alcohol also boosted my confidence. I worried less what other people thought about me and would wonder: *why does it play on both sides? Why does it boost my ego but also reduce my thoughts?*

Like alcohol, there are many external sources that could rid me of my mind for a short period. Sex, drugs, alcohol and adrenaline-based activities always made me feel as though I was free, totally present and living in pure happiness. I would delve into them too frequently, though, turning the freedom on its tail. I'd never get what I was looking for: a less-frantic mind.

This high had lower lows.

Taking drugs took me away from my loud thoughts. My mind would rest for a short period, giving me that elated sense of freedom. Partaking in these freedom-giving activities, though, made me feel trapped. My ego was resting, building up strength, then once the drug high was over my negative thoughts would be back in full force against my now-fragile mind and depleted body caused by the chemicals streaming through it and not a second's sleep in days. The thoughts would come back with full power and my weakened mind would be drained of any serotonin, the happiness chemical. It would be no match for the rested ego looking for stimulation. My soft body and having no food or sleep for days would compound my vulnerability.

Regret, fear, depression and tears would settle in as my mind continued teasing my misfortune.

This high had lower lows.

During sex I was totally present, not a worry in the world. I had company, I was happy. After sex I would feel lonely if my partner was asleep or gone. I would lie there worrying about my performance, the evil ego bellowing in laughter and leaving me feeling dejected. A lack of sex, too, frustrated my anxious, built-up body.

This high had lower lows.

Adrenaline-based activities were euphoric, a feeling I would search for time and again. After such a high, everyday life seemed dull. I would take more daring risks to top the exhilaration from the previous high.

All these highs had even lower lows.

Ignoring the ego is not the same as letting go of it. If you close a bedroom door to a room on fire hoping it will go away you will soon be burned.

Presence comes from within, so why was I given these glimpses of presence in external sources, resulting in the opposite of what I was looking for? Was I being shown the possibilities of a present and peaceful mind? Why, then, was it taken and replaced with a turbulent, violent and noisy one?

Was I being punished for looking for happiness somewhere other than within? Like rummaging for reading glasses only to find them sitting on my head. Searching for something I already had seemed comical.

Until it drove me mad.

I looked past Ruben, who was asleep, through the window at a pitch black sky. I was bored. I watched Ruben for a few moments then, giggling, flicked his face and quickly turned away, pretending I didn't do anything.

'You're fucked. Stop that shit,' Ruben said without opening his eyes.

'Wake up, you prick, I'm bored,' I responded. He didn't budge.

I gripped the top of the headrest in front of me to assist raising myself out of my chair.

'Ow!' I heard from in front. As well as the headrest, I'd clenched a bunch of a lady's hair.

'Sorry about that,' I mumbled, standing tall. I stood in the aisle and looked down at the lady I had just hurt.

'I'm really sorry.' I hoped for an acquittal.

'It's okay,' she responded while fixing her hair, some of which was covering her face. I stumbled down the aisles of the plane. The odd reading light remained on, blurring my vision a little. Couples were leaning on each other while asleep, and a businessman was intently focused on his laptop and typing away. A young girl was asleep over her father's lap, and he looked up at me and smiled. I gave a drunken wink in reply.

This is boring, I thought as I turned to head back to my seat. I sat down and pushed the service button to get another drink.

'Sir, you press too much.' The Thai flight attendants were sick of me pushing my button for drinks. 'We leave bottle out,' she whispered, not wanting to further disrupt the plane full of people. They ended up leaving the bottle of Hennessy behind a curtain for me to pour my own. I remembered hearing stories of Australian sport stars drinking copious amounts of alcohol on flights, so I decided to tally my own.

At 16 Hennessy and lemonades I lost count.

I heard a frustrated sigh come from Ruben as I spilled some of my drink onto my lap. 'Let's chill out and watch this,' he said in a defeated, tired tone. In an attempt to settle me down Ruben put the movie *Borat* on for us to watch. I rolled my drunken eyes and sat staring at the screen, my mind racing. I could see Ruben looking over at me through the corner of his eyes.

This is shit, my thoughts raced. *He said we were going to have fun on this trip. He's boring.* The cacophonous sound of my mind continued to bounce through the walls of my head. It felt like a casino floor with every slot machine going off at once, spitting coins, bells ringing, sirens blaring and people screaming. My thoughts were at differing levels, each one trying to outdo the previous one. Then one would pop in to play the mediator.

Alright, let's settle down. Just chill out and wait until we get there to be stupid, my better thoughts reasoned.

The movie idea was working. I sat quietly, to the outside world, that is. While I was watching the movie my jaw started to shift a little. My incessant mind started to play out in the physical form and I could feel myself getting agitated. My knee started rocking a little. I noticed Ruben moving around a little in his chair after picking up on my anxious energy. *Just relax, just chill out. Watch the movie.* My mind tried to settle.

It worked . . . a little.

I can't take this any more! my mind screamed. *Here we go. Fuck this silence rubbish.*

What am I: a fucking librarian or something?

'Not!' I yelled at the top of my lungs, startling the entire plane full of people.

In the movie Borat kept saying 'Not!' in an intense way; I simply aped him. 'Not! Not! Not!' I shouted, imitating the movie. Ruben grabbed at my shoulder and tried to put his hand over my mouth.

I laughed uncontrollably.

The lady sitting across the aisle from me woke and mumbled something under her breath before facing the other direction.

'Will you stop that!' The lady whose hair I had pulled had turned and was propped up in her seat.

'What?' I slurred back.

'You are putting your knee into the back of my seat. Stop it!' she growled. She'd had enough.

'Chill out, will you,' I said back, as if she was the annoying one.

The flight was tedious, and after countless amounts of drinks I was getting annoyed myself about having to visit the toilet every 10 minutes. Hours ticked by, and my impatience rose. I shifted in my seat uncontrollably and rubbed the top of my head with my hands like I always did when I got frustrated. Even though I was still drinking, the buzz from the alcohol was wearing off. If I didn't have to keep going to the toilet I would've passed out.

The plane finally touched down, and before the seatbelt sign was off people were standing to grab their carry-on luggage. I stayed slumped in my chair, a little exhausted after the long flight. 'That was the worst,' I said to Ruben. 'I hate flying.'

He just stared at me.

The plane felt muggy, and people stomped past me with tired eyes. There wasn't a smile between the lot of them.

'Miserable bastards,' I whispered to Ruben.

'It's your fault, bro. Everyone is tired and angry because of you. All you did was fuck around,' he said, shaking his head.

'Who cares?' I responded. 'I didn't mean any harm. I was just mucking around.' I'd often play the innocent one after mucking up, hoping to get someone on my side to make me feel better. If I didn't get anyone on my side I'd keep drinking to lessen my concerns. 'Who gives a shit, anyway? We're in Bangkok!'

Chapter 3

STUMBLING INTO A NEW WORLD

Thursday, 20 November

We landed at Bangkok around midnight, then collected our bags and walked towards the exit doors. I dragged my bag behind me, and it clapped occasionally as its wheels bounced over people's feet. The electric doors opened up to Thailand. Beep! Beep! Horns blared. The muggy heat seemed suffocating, or maybe it was the thick pollution.

'Hey, where you go? Best taxi. Cheapest,' a local man standing to my right and dressed in a dirty blue-collared shirt enquired.

'My taxi air-conditioning,' another butted in from our left, his half tucked-in shirt looking scrappy. My head snapped left to right trying to take it all in.

A man standing with a whistle and waving his arms screamed out in his native tongue, marshalling the traffic. It was manic, but under control.

Wow, we are here, I thought. Walking out into the busy street signalled to me the start of our adventure. I was in Thailand with my brother, and with no rules. I could do what I wanted. We were mobbed by a few more taxi drivers who were looking for our business.

It would take an hour by taxi to get to Pattaya, which is a beautiful little strip along the coastline although it mirrored Sydney's Kings Cross with shows, drugs and people from all walks of life.

'I need a beer first,' Ruben said. He walked back inside as I stood mesmerised by the chaos.

This trip is going to be insane, I thought. *We can do whatever we want. I wouldn't mind training as well while we're here. I can fight some of their local fighters. Lucky I brought my mouthguard.*

'My mouthguard,' I whispered to myself. I bent down and started rummaging through my bag, slipping the guard into my pocket as Ruben returned.

'Let's go,' he said, a little less tense as he took the first sip of his beer.

We hopped into a taxi. We yelled out in stupidity in the back seat, and noticed the driver looking a little nervous as we carried on.

'Hey!' I yelled at him. He didn't budge. 'Hey!' I said again, this time grabbing his shirt.

He turned abruptly, taking his eyes off the road. 'Don't touch,' he said, a silver blade in his left hand revealing itself and sparkling as a passing car's lights illuminated it.

Silence.

The driver kept his eyes on me as the taxi sped down the road. I had a choice to make: do I aggravate the situation, or do I diffuse it? It was never a thing of being scared. I had been faced with this type of situation before, having been stabbed after attacking another person who had pulled a knife on me. Why was I the aggressor on those occasions? My ego. I had people around me at the time who would have doubted me if I didn't attack.

Knowing Ruben was more intent on partying than fighting, my mind quickly determined my response. It was as though I would float out of my body and scan the immediate surroundings, even myself. I'd then contemplate every reaction, summing it all up to figure out and produce my next move. My floating, arbitrating self locked on to Ruben. *What will he say if I don't attack?*

Knowing Ruben would be happy if I didn't fight, like a checkout chick scanning groceries, my thoughts moved on to the next item to scan. *What will the driver think? Who cares, I will never see him again.* My mind quickly dismissed his opinion.

With my mind finishing scanning the car's items, I produced the total.

'Want a beer?' I asked the driver as I motioned to pass him one.

He placed the knife down on the front passenger's seat, smiled and grabbed the beer.

As he sipped his drink, with not a nerve in sight, we proceeded to our destination.

Without anybody to show off to, I backed down. A peaceful outcome. Had I been with someone from my crew or another person who loved to fight this taxi ride could have been deadly.

It was 2 am when we arrived in Pattaya. Ruben and I checked into our hotel, and though the hour was late sleep was never a thought in our minds. Dumping our bags in our room, we hit the town.

Pattaya's main street runs along a coast filled with beautiful resorts, run-down buildings, shops and bars covered in bright fluorescent lights and plenty of desperate tourists walking around looking for a lady friend. The fresh salty scent of the Andaman Sea was occasionally interrupted by the stench of discarded food, unsold and left to rot from a nearby market stall. Where the street closed off to cars it was packed with people selling everything you can think of: photos with animals, food, suits, fake jewellery, weapons, drugs and also themselves.

We confidently walked into a small door that led into a shabby building and headed downstairs. It opened into what looked like a massive cave. The calmness of the entrance was smashed into oblivion as lights flickered and coloured lasers combed the room. Smoke was everywhere, occasionally separating as a sexy dancer's arm glided through it. The music's bass was pumping as clubbers' heads bounced to the beat.

This place was incredible.

'Bro, what the fuck! This is crazy!' I screamed above the music at Ruben's smiling face.

I danced as Ruben looked at me and motioned with his hands to imitate drinking out of a cup. I nodded my head, accepting his offer of a drink. He disappeared into the crowd.

I stood with a grin on my face as he returned and handed me a drink. Grabbing it intently, I spilled a little onto my hand.

I sipped my drink as I started to dance and noticed Ruben looking at me, laughing. I was used to dancing at raves, not clubs, so my dance moves weren't the best. I had a twinkling of absolute pleasure as I decided that I was glad I had come on this trip. That moment summed up the reason for most of my partying ventures: dancing, laughing, drinking and an opportunity to hook up with a female.

I finished my first drink and was heading towards the bar to get another when Ruben grabbed me. 'Let's get out of here,' he said.

'No way, this is the best!' I thought he was joking.

'There's another good spot down the road.'

'Man, why did we leave there?' I complained as we walked back outside. We were only in the club for 20 minutes but the energy outside on the streets felt like it had disappeared, leaving behind an atmosphere that was decaying by the second: tourists passed out on the ground, one vomiting in the gutter as his friends watched on laughing, business owners closing up their shops with their eyes half open. It started to drop my spirits a little.

'Why did we leave?' I asked again.

'Yeah, we probably should have stayed,' Ruben said, his voice a little slurred as he glanced around at the barren streets. 'I wanted to show you a better spot, but it's closed.'

The incessant mind at work. Even though we were in an incredible spot Ruben's mind wasn't content and it needed more feeding, more validation by showing me he knew all the spots. I couldn't be mad at him because I would have done the same. Wherever I was I could feel relaxed for only a few moments before I'd decide I needed to be somewhere else – convincing myself that the reason I felt unsettled was because of the location. A lot of times I would go somewhere else but end up regretting I hadn't stayed at the first spot, which then magnified how unsettled I was.

'Let's go back to the first spot,' I said as Ruben was already turning around to do so.

As we walked into the club a petite local woman was leaving, and we caught each other's eyes and smiled. Nothing was said before we were in each other's arms.

'See you back at the room,' Ruben called over his shoulder as he kept walking into the club. My new friend and I headed in the other direction.

I stumbled off arm in arm with this stranger and we hopped into a taxi. It was a pickup truck with a back tray that had a roof but no sides and it was lined with seats on either side. Most of the taxis were. When we got back to the hotel I was approached by a staff member. Apparently you had to pay to take someone back to your room. This was money a drunken fool would be happy to part with, a fool like me.

I closed the door to my room and turned to see my new friend already undressing herself. I'm sure this would excite most men in this situation, but it did the opposite to me. I loved the thrill of the chase and then an eventual romantic date. This was too easy; it felt rehearsed, boring. Back home I'd see a beautiful lady on the street and approach her for a conversation. I loved the freshness of such an encounter, and if it was in front of a bunch of my friends even better. It was a fun risk, a chance she might tell me to go away or give me her number to meet up again another time.

More often than not I'd get the phone number. Halve that again for the amount of times I actually called. It wasn't about getting a date – that's not what I wanted – it was the feeling of success and the ego boost from winning. Winning the game of picking up. I'd talk to the boys about it and loved a back slap. It was another prime example of the mind preferring to want than to have.

If I were to go on the date I enjoyed a night of deep conversation, a passionate kiss and the possibility of taking it further.

The whole process – the picking up in the street, chatting over the phone, organising a date, getting through the setback of a postponed date, organising a nice location, shopping for a new outfit, preparing with a fresh haircut, buying a bottle of wine after guessing what type she would like, tidying up my bedroom in case she would come home, the butterflies moments before going in for a first kiss – all this sort of stuff was like a challenge. Most times, without even fully knowing the person, we'd sleep together. Afterwards, I'd lie staring at the ceiling feeling completely empty. There were occasions when a tear would run down my face as I had a stranger tucked under my arms. All the planning, preparing, anticipation, talking about it to my boys and showing off who I was about to take out, all of it, all the energy, for what? To be left empty, to have opened a beautiful woman's heart only for me to be in my head and regretting every part of it. It wasn't right.

I'd lie to myself leading up to a date by telling myself that there may be potential for me to actually start dating the person as a possible partner, knowing full well deep inside that it wasn't what I wanted. I could kid myself, but when it was all done the truth would be revealed. On a first date there were also possibilities of us not connecting, of neither of us being into it.

There was none of that there in my hotel room. I walked over to the bed and kicked my shorts free of my feet as she, completely naked, leaned back on the bed.

A few minutes in, I looked down and noticed the condom had snapped. My body froze, a million scenarios entering my mind. HIV jumped to the front of all the stories. I freaked out, screamed and swore and ran straight for the shower. In the shower in a stupid and urgent attempt to rid myself of any chance of catching something I scrubbed away.

I heard the door to my room close.

I walked out of the bathroom dripping wet to an empty room, and sat down on the side of the bed naked. I poured another rum from my tax-free supply.

Lie down or run at it? I contemplated.

I threw my glass back, downing its contents, then I exited the room.

Out and about, I headed back to the main street of Pattaya to look for Ruben. It was then around 4 am, and I was wandering around without a clue where I was going. I couldn't find him anywhere. I wasn't too fussed; I could do what I wanted.

Beep! A loud horn startled me as I went to step off the footpath onto the road. The car had just missed me. Stumbling back onto the footpath, I saw a man out of the corner of my eye head straight over to me. I turned so I wouldn't get caught off guard, and in front of me stood a scummy-looking, unshaven Thai man. He had a thick, long black hair coming out of a mole on his chin, which I stared at as he began a sentence.

'You want drug, you want drug?' he spoke out of the side of his crummy mouth. This was exactly how it looked when a news report back home showed how Thailand was rife with drugs and drug set-ups. *'Fuck going there,'* Dad would comment on the story.

If I hadn't already consumed a bottle shop–worth of alcohol I would've turned and walked in the other direction.

'Fuck, yeah, I do. What you got?' was my dumb response.

'What you want?' he smiled, realising he had a potential customer.

'You got coke?' I asked hopefully.

He nodded his head as he pulled out three satchels from his pocket. Each satchel's contents varied in colour, from pale white to a pasty yellow.

'One thousand baht,' he said. I did a mental calculation and realised that the coke was just under $40 Australian. In Australia I'd paid an average of $350 per gram. My eyes lit up.

Instead of just accepting his offer, I tried my hand at bargaining with the man. I'd heard you could bargain down just about anything here on the street.

'Nah, bullshit, I'll give you five hundred,' I said.

We stood in the main street, his arm extending and his fingers indicating the automatic two-year minimum gaol sentence.

His short fingers gave off the impression they were that of a child's, though the contents they held belonged to a devil's advocate.

Most people bargained for cheaper DVDs or fake shirts. I wanted a cheaper prison term.

'No, one thousand!' he angrily said.

'Fuck you, I'm not getting it then.' I attempted to bluff my way into the deal, even though I knew full well I would have paid double what he was asking in the first place, especially back home.

People walking past glanced over. I looked at them with my cloudy eyes and smiled, the severity of possible outcomes not entering my mind as I was so intent on furthering my high, on escaping more from the moment. Someone in that crowd could have been a cop or a person eager to warn the authorities, but no one bothered me and the attention pushed me further. It felt good.

'Seven fifty,' I demanded.

'Okay,' he said as he snatched my money.

I blindly grabbed a satchel out of his hands, took off with my purchase and stuck it between my butt cheeks. As I ran up dark back lanes I didn't look back. My fast run turned into a light jog as I cruised past a crowd of people. Sweat dripped off my eyelids as my heart thumped from the short sprint and the anxiety caused by the thought of getting caught with drugs in Thailand. I hoped I wouldn't be tackled from behind and arrested. The hotel was getting closer and I knew my stupid risk had paid off.

At the door to our room I could hear people having sex. I entered anyway. Ruben was with a tall, dark-skinned lady. They both glanced over at me, stopping for a second, but then went straight back to their moaning.

I sat on a chair near the bed, watching, my thoughts racing. *Do they care that I'm here? Should I leave? Nah, let's get another drink. Wait!* I recalled what I had firmly embedded between my butt cheeks.

'Hey, brother, look what I've got.' I reached down the back of my pants. They both stopped to look at me as I showed what I had. I held the small satchel in one hand while I flicked it with the other, then I giggled.

'What the fuck is that?' roared Ruben.

'Coke,' I said, as I smacked it on the bench near the television. He came straight over.

'You fucking dickhead! Are you serious? Where'd you get it?' He pushed me and I rocked on my feet.

'Relax, brother, I got it off this little scummy guy,' I said, regaining my balance and hoping my detailed description of the dealer would lessen his worries.

'They might have followed you here!' Ruben said as he rushed over to the door, keeping his naked body inside while poking his head out.

'Nah, I ran, it's all good.' I said to lessen his concerns and settle him down. His worry soon turned to excitement as I lined out my purchase. Excitement soon turned back to worry when we both realised it was a light green colour instead of coke's usual pearly white.

After a brief thought of not consuming any, the good old alcohol took over and I bent down to suck this mystery substance up my nose.

With the alcohol diminishing my ability to taste I couldn't be sure, but I didn't want Ruben to have another cry. I commented while still sniffing residue: 'Yep, it's good.'

It worked. Ruben sniffed his line.

'Can I have one?' Ruben's buddy asked in an African accent, still naked on the bed.

'Of course you can, come here,' I said, holding out the rolled-up Aussie banknote to her. She approached the bench and reached out to take the note. Within a whisker of her grabbing it I yelled out, imitating Borat, 'Not!' I pulled the note towards my own nose and sucked in a second line.

Ruben and I burst into drunken laughter.

He held onto my shoulder, connecting us in the moment. We were unsteady on our feet, so we dropped to our knees. We couldn't stop laughing.

Breaking through our reverie, the woman snapped in a deep tone, 'Fuck you!'

'I'm only playing, come here,' I said, trying to call a truce as I knocked out another line of coke.

She must have not liked Borat because she left the room pissed off.

Her deep tone and anger-filled bark stopped our laughter. It was far from a joke.

Realising she was disgruntled had punched my mind with fear. *What if she goes to the cops?*

She might know heaps of bad people here. We could get fucked over. I glanced over at Ruben, and the worried look on his face told me he was having the same scary thoughts.

It was a damned stupid move, one of many made on this trip. It would be incredibly easy for a disgruntled woman to go straight to the police and tell them of our activities.

Ruben was ready to call it a night but I wasn't. The cocktail of alcohol and drugs in my system dictated my actions. 'I'm going out to get a bite to eat,' I announced. Ever since I had started my exercise regime getting drunk meant getting extra hungry, and tonight was no exception.

'Bullshit, bro, pull up man,' Ruben pleaded.

'Fuck that, I'm going. Let me take your camera: I'll get some photos.' I'd get plenty of ideas when drinking, ideas I thought were smart at the time. Thinking I could get any photos in this state was one of the stupider ones.

'No way in the world are you taking my new camera.'

'Come on, I'll be back soon,' I said, squinting my eyes a little to imitate annoyance.

'No!' he said as he lay down.

'Fuck you, then,' I slurred.

I wanted the camera but Ruben wouldn't let me have it. My chance came: the moment his head hit the pillow he was snoring.

I left the room . . . with the camera.

As I stumbled down a side alley to the main street I could see a tall lady's silhouette heading towards me. As she walked past I felt a slight touch on my leg. I reached down to my pocket and a sudden jolt of realisation stopped me dead still. As I turned I shouted 'Motherfucker, give it back!' The bitch had taken my wallet. I swear to this day the touch I felt was no more than a kiss of wind. This pickpocket was good!

She jumped on the back of a motorised scooter on which her accomplice was waiting. I yelled at the top of my lungs as I ran after them both: 'Ah, motherfucker!'

I was a man on a mission, storming towards the bike and my fists pumping through the air as I gained momentum. The scooter was slow to take off and I got within 1 metre of it.

The bitch threw my wallet. I stopped and bent down to pick it up as they turned a corner to make their escape. The money was gone. I didn't care, though, about the money; I was just happy to get my wallet full of my identification back. Most of my funds were in card form, so they didn't get too much.

I walked the near-empty streets pissed off at just being robbed. It wasn't the fact that I had lost money that made me angry, it was more that it felt like I lost – that the other person won and they got one over me. The ego doesn't like defeat. My mind convinced me that because they outsmarted me I was less of a person, that their mind-made identity was stronger than mine.

'Can't believe that piece of shit! How'd I let it happen? You're better than that. Fucking hell. Dog! Wish I caught her,' I whispered to myself, shaking my head with each remark. I noticed two local men to my left staring at me with concerned looks on their faces. I guess they were a little worried about the drunk foreigner storming up the street talking to himself. When angry my loud mind would play out in the physical form, my thoughts so built up, energised and multiplied they would force themselves out of my mouth. Sometimes when a heavy thought popped into my head, without consciously doing it my head would shake rapidly to try to rid my mind of the thought.

'What the fuck are you doing?' a friend of mine said to me one day after seeing the head tremor.

'Just happens from time to time,' I laughed.

After getting some funds from an ATM I walked into a small bar and ordered two shots of vodka. I downed those faster than the pickpocket had grabbed my wallet and was back to feeling better about the trip. I ordered two more shots, and after downing those the last thing I remember was placing the empty shot glass on the bar.

Chapter 4

JUST . . . BE . . .
SILENT . . .

Friday, 21 November

'Where's my camera, where's my camera?' Ruben's voice was the first thing I heard the following morning. I was back in the hotel room. Naked.

'Where's my camera?' he said again.

'What camera?' I slurred.

'You fuck! You took my camera.' He pushed at me harder.

I had blacked out. It wasn't something that happened often, but whenever it did I thought of it as my mind's way of saying 'Mate, you don't want to see what you're up to now. You're fucking right up, I'm out of here.'

Like my consciousness a few hours earlier, the camera was gone.

To black out in Thailand was stupid. Ruben said I returned at 6 am completely wasted after being out for a couple of hours. Being woken by Ruben's complaints smashed my body with tension and anxiety. The morning after a big night, especially after a blackout and not remembering what I had gotten up to, my body would shake a little and my mind would start with the regret, fear and paranoia.

How much cash did I spend? My knuckles are okay, so I didn't fight. I hope I didn't. What if I hurt someone? What's that scratch on my leg from? You lost his camera. Why did I take it? I wish I hadn't taken it! Hope I didn't message Anne back home. What if I broke the law here and got locked up! Fuck, that would be bad. That African lady: no! What if she comes back?

'Bro, you're fucked!' Ruben was still going on about his camera, so I poured a rum from my second bottle. I felt sorry for myself and the rum soon made me feel better.

'You fuck!! That camera was twelve hundred!'

Trying to settle him down I said, 'I'll buy you one, bro.' My mind teased, telling me that I had ruined the trip. I felt depressed but put on a brave face. 'Screw it, let's go get breakfast. Make me feel better.'

'Fuck the food, you lost my camera!' Ruben screamed.

I sighed. 'Mate, I'm sorry. I'll get you a new one. Let's go eat.'

We walked down the streets of Pattaya to look for some western food. Indian men were already standing on the footpath outside their stores trying to sell suits.

'Soot, soot,' a tall Indian man said as he grabbed me and attempted to put his arm around my shoulder.

'Fuck off, I don't want a suit!' I was still drunk and anxious, and wasn't in any mood for someone grabbing my arm trying to sell me something.

'McDonald's: yes!' It was as foreign as I was. It was weird seeing the big, shiny golden arches with English writing among the scrappiness and rundown stores selling knockoff clothes. It looked out of place.

'Reckon they have normal shit here? I said to Ruben as we walked up a couple of steps to enter.

'What do you mean?'

'Well, I don't want a fucking red curry burger and pad Thai chips.'

'You dick,' he giggled. 'They've got all the normal stuff.'

As we reached the top of the stairs to the entrance of McDonald's I noticed two female employees looking at us, laughing. I smirked back as we walked inside.

I went to the counter to order and looked at some of the food on the menu. There were burgers, but the patties looked different.

'Bro, what is this shit?' I asked Ruben.

'Relax, they've got normal stuff too.'

I glanced around the restaurant, and every staff member stopped what they were doing to look at us. A man tossing fries who was dressed differently from the others and was wearing a blue-collared shirt approached us. I guessed he was the manager.

'Oh, drunk man, drunk man!' he said, pointing at me. 'You very drunk in here before, very loud. You don't remember?'

Oh no, I thought, staring at him. Ruben stood there confused. I was shocked; I didn't know what to say.

'Ah, sorry, I can't remember anything. I hope I wasn't too bad,' I replied, squinting my face to amplify my concern.

He chuckled. 'You wait here.' He walked into a back room.

He was gone for about one minute and paranoia set in. It was something that always happened after a night on drugs or alcohol. I would worry uncontrollably after a bender as I could never really remember what I had done. My mind and body were so brittle, my ego would shine and take over every emotion and make me tremble in fear. It was near impossible to think positive thoughts to cheer myself up after a big night. I would watch something uplifting on television in an attempt to calm myself, though my mind would still creep in and introduce something to worry about. Maybe a mean character would die in the cartoon I was watching. Something as clean as a cartoon could remind me about death, which resulted in me losing my breath from worrying about my own demise.

My mind would search for anything to be felt. The emotion of fear is the easiest to find and one of the most action-packed for a hungry yet brittle mind. The mind loves stimulation. When I was vulnerable after a night out it would soon find it. Often the morning after a bender I would get on the drugs and drink again to delay the depression. In the end, though, it would only get worse.

I was paranoid about the manager calling the police because I may have mucked up. 'Let's get out of here, bro,' I said, and we started to walk out.

'Sir, sir, stop!' I heard from behind. We both stopped and slowly turned around to see the manager coming from the back room holding something in his hand.

'The camera, you're joking!' I hollered.

He smiled and handed it to me. We couldn't believe it. I know back in Australia 99 times out of 100 if you lose something then it was as good as gone. To return something to a person who was no doubt being a total moron only a couple hours earlier just goes to show what an amazing man this manager was.

I gave him a $100 Australian bill. 'Worth very much, worth very much,' I said, speaking to him like he was a two year old.

'I know, thank you,' he said softly through a smile as he cupped his hands together, slowly lowered his eyelids and gave a bow of his head.

We were delirious as we walked out of McDonald's, still not believing we got the camera back from a chance visit to get breakfast. A huge bout of guilt had been lifted off me. We decided to celebrate, and over a couple of drinks we looked through the camera. It was full of photos of me posing with Thai ladies and eating McDonald's.

To this day I have no idea who was holding the camera.

After downing a couple more drinks we decided we were hungry again so we went to an all you can eat buffet. I was drinking more than I was eating and Ruben started getting annoyed at my stupidity again.

Trips to Thailand had been a regular thing for Ruben. He was used to partying there but also chilling out and enjoying the country.

'Bro, I didn't know you would be carrying on this bad,' Ruben said, exhausted. He was already doubting his decision to take me as his holidaying partner as I was turning into a liability. We left the restaurant, and as we walked down the main street we were approached by a man selling tiny rubber penises.

Ruben told him to go away, but I decided to buy one so I could throw it at people. By the 10th local I'd pissed off by hitting them with this rubber penis Ruben had had enough.

'Fucking pull up!' Ruben said through his teeth as he grabbed me by my shoulder and pulled me close to him. 'I knew I shouldn't have brought you! Look, you are pissing everyone off,' he said, pointing in the direction of four Thai men and one lady standing close by and staring at us with angry looks on their faces.

'Who cares? Relax, man, I'm only mucking around.'

'You're a dickhead,' he said as he released his grip and pushed me.

'Don't fucking push me.' Now I was angry. I could let things slide and laugh at him getting angry but after a while I would snap. We would be close to blows at least once per month, although the next day it would be as if nothing had happened. I didn't like keeping grudges with him.

'I'm going to do some shopping. You do your best and I'll meet up with you at the hotel in a few hours,' he demanded.

'Sweet!' I responded, happy to hear his request.

He was sick of me but I was even more annoyed with his efforts to calm me down. I went straight back to the hotel to have some more rum.

At the time I didn't know why I always wanted to keep drinking. It wasn't until later that I understood.

I sat alone in the room as I thought about my next move. I felt a little twitch in my nose before it started burning. It felt clogged up and was soon scorching in pain. I blew my nose and green and yellow muck came out mixed with blood. My dice with the green coke had me worried.

Nothing a rum couldn't fix.

I ventured back out into the hot midday sun looking for adventure.

'Soot, soot.' Another Indian man with blond streaks through his dusty, dirt-brown hair approached me. 'You want custom soot? Very cheap, best material,' he attempted.

I was sick of these guys, but being in a jovial mood I entered his 2 by 2 metre shop and told him I'd get something. I wasn't in the mood to get measured up, so I reasoned with the guy.

'I don't want a suit but I still want to buy something off you.' I left with a tie around my neck.

As I strutted down Pattaya's footpaths in nothing but sandals, a pair of short shorts, a singlet and a tie I was getting some weird looks.

'Hey, mister, nice tie,' I heard from my right in broken English. My ego was loving the attention and I was feeding it.

I attempted to stop a taxi, though the driver was looking in the other direction as he flew past. I looked to see what he was staring at. My eyes were caught off guard as it felt as though I was staring directly at the sun. Using my hand to shield some of the glare, I realised the blinding rays of the sun were beaming off a golden statue. To the side large concrete stairs seemed to lead up to and disappear into the sky. I walked a little closer, and doing so changed the angle of the sun so I could see what the statue was. It was Buddha.

I was ignorant of any religion besides Christianity at that point. I knew Buddha was the man whose fat stomach you rubbed for luck, but that was the extent of my religious education. Even though I claimed to be Christian I had no real grasp on the stories of Jesus or the Bible. I claimed Christianity as a safeguard, hoping that my possession of the religion would allow me to live after death. Much later in life Christ came deeply into my father's heart and then mine.

I hesitated. The stairway to the heavens looked inviting but I wanted to remain monogamous to my religion, so I turned to walk away. I cheated on girlfriends, not my chance at heaven.

As I turned a bald Western man wearing an orange robe brushed past me as he headed towards the stairs. Even though he barely touched me, I felt as though the wind left in his wake was pulling me towards him. I was intoxicated and more than likely still affected by drugs, so I doubted my senses. He stopped at the bottom of the stairs, the sun's reflection sparkling off his hair-free head. He stood there at the base of the stairs as though waiting for me, and I felt an incredible amount of energy building up in my stomach. Before I realised it I was walking in his direction. He had his back to me as I reached out to tap him on the shoulder and ask him what this place was.

'Just be silent,' he said without turning around.

He had pretty much told me to shut up, but whatever urge I would normally have to lash out was washed away. His words echoed with a frequency in my being. The way he said those three words 'Just . . . be . . . silent . . .' was like each word was coming from its own Tibetan singing bowl.

Ding.

Just.

Ding.

Be.

Ding.

Silent.

Each time one of the bowls was tapped the energy of the word covered my aura, silencing me.

Ding.

Just.

Ding.

Be.

Ding.

Silent.

He looked like he was gliding up the stairs with zero effort, almost as though he was on an escalator. His feet soundlessly landed on each step as he gracefully ascended, while my sandals slapped hard against the concrete in contrast. Sweat dripped off my eyebrows and I could feel the sun burning my skin. I wiped my forehead with my tie as I was overtaken by a tour group being led by a lady in a collared shirt, who herself was being ushered by a monk.

'Local people come here to pay their respects and pray for health, happiness and wealth, among other things.'

Wouldn't mind all of those myself, I thought as I listened in on the tour. I looked back up the stairs, and even though the sun was shining down on me from above it looked like *another* sun was rising at the top of the stairs. It seemed like a blinding pile of gold was sitting at the top, enticing people to push through on the last leg of the monstrous stairs. I stopped to catch my breath and wondered what happened to my Western monk who, by example alone, pulled me up those stairs. Had he continued on his path knowing his job had been done? As I got closer the huge gold pile revealed itself to be another statue, this time of a skinny person sitting crossed legged and meditating. With a final flap of my sandal I stood tall, observing my surroundings. I smiled. Something about this place had left me feeling energised.

'This Buddha statue has been here for over fifty years,' I heard the tour guide say.

My mind started to wander, as it tended to do, and I wondered what I was even doing there in the first place listening to the tour guide.

Why am I listening? I thought to myself.

I rarely listened. Even when meeting someone I'd be in my head.

'Hi, Luke, I'm . . ., we met at . . .' was all I would hear when someone introduced themselves. Words were muffled out by my thoughts.

How do I know this person? Should I know them? Do they know I don't know who they are? Fuck, what was their name? Did they just ask a question? Hope I don't have anything in my teeth.

I had onion at lunch; chuck a piece of chewing gum in your mouth. Shit, I don't have any left. Stand back.

'It was nice to meet you, Luke.'

'You too, mate.'

Just . . . be . . . silent . . .

Those three words vibrated again through my aura, a reminder.

She's got no idea, I thought, glaring at the slim statue. My thoughts were back in full force. *Buddha is fat, there's no way that's Buddha.* My ego jumped in to question what the guide was saying. I rarely trusted any information, as my ego thought it knew better.

I walked closer to the statue, pushing aside my doubts. A plaque at its base stated it was indeed Buddha. I was confused. All I knew about Buddha was that he was a big fat man.

Just . . . be . . . silent . . .

I stopped myself and decided to listen intently on the tour, to try to make sense of it all.

'The Buddhists meditate daily, they do this to relax,' the guide stated.

The monk who was shepherding the group reached out to touch the tour guide gently on her wrist, and she stopped speaking.

The group hadn't seemed to be paying much attention up until that point, and they stopped chatting among themselves to stare at the old Thai man in his orange robe.

The monk, by presence alone, commanded attention.

'We don't *do* meditation,' he said, emphasising the word 'do' as he stood in the shadow of the golden Buddha statue. 'Meditation is who we are when we live our mind, can go very fast, thinking,' he continued in his humble broken English.

'When our minds so busy we aren't who we are. When meditating the mind is silent. That is who we are. We are pure being.'

When I heard him say those words, suddenly my spirit knew what he meant. I felt the words go over my body and tell me this was truth. Back home, whenever I visited a church I couldn't understand what was being said; it was like the priest was speaking in code. My mind would try to understand what was going on. The mind attempts with its past conditioning to analyse itself into opening up to spirit. When you let go of the mind and have faith, that's when your heart is filled with a deep knowing rather than a belief.

A silent mind, I wondered. My mind was forever frantic. *Is it possible to escape from this?*

I strolled away as a slight wind cooled my burning face, and I looked up into the sky. I felt . . . happy. I hadn't really thought about it much, with the travelling and the partying, but my life over the last year had really improved immensely. And in that moment I imagined my life getting even better, especially if there was a possibility to shut my thoughts up.

Where are these good thoughts and feelings coming from? Was the slowing down of my mind allowing my true self to shine? I've gotta hold on to this feeling! When I get home I'm going to start meditating more, I thought. *People will laugh at you, bro. Fuck 'em, who cares? Yeah, but you're a boxer, you can't do that soft stuff.*

Again, I tried to use my mind to understand why I was feeling good, which then projected forward to predict what else may happen. With this the seesaw was back in full force and those good feelings were gone.

I liked to control and understand, and in doing so my soul, which can't be controlled or understood, would be suffocated.

I imagined myself wearing the same orange robe as the monk. *Maybe I should try church again. Could I do both?* I'll admit I was an extremist with anything I found myself getting into, but I wanted to further improve my life after coming so far from my turbulent past. I was searching.

Just breathe, bro. I got out of my head and focused on my breath.

I started walking down the stairs, and this time there was no flapping of my sandal. My feet softly touched the concrete steps and I felt lighter. Occasionally I brushed the sandstone railing with my fingertips as I descended to the street, everything feeling like it had slowed down. My head felt spacious, and with a slight grin raised on my lips I felt peaceful.

I was silent.

The moment I reached the bottom of the stairs I was met with beeping horns as I tripped on a crack in the footpath. It was like I had stepped out of a beautiful weightless dream into a thunderous cloudy funeral. My mind switched instantly to wondering what I should do now. My feet slapped on the ground again as I was weighed down with thought. I was thirsty from the big stairs and searing heat so I decided to quench my thirst with more alcohol.

Sitting in a footpath bar, I took my last mouthful of rum. It was my third drink in five minutes. The ice cubes were rattling against each other as I held the cup to my mouth, making sure I didn't leave any drink behind. I looked down the cup at a footpath full of new motorbikes.

I loved riding bikes, and a shiny red one caught my eye. I hopped off the barstool and stumbled over. I slid my hand across the unblemished petrol tank as I looked it over, then a stout, 4 feet–tall woman walked up behind me. 'You want to ride this bike?' she asked.

'Yeah, I ride bikes back home. Why? You know who owns it?' I asked.

'I do,' she replied.

'So, you ride bikes?' I slurred the words and realised I needed to speak clearer to hide my intoxicated state. I wanted to ride that bike. 'You don't look like a rider,' I said more deeply.

'We all ride bike here. You rent from me,' she responded.

I was a little confused. She noticed this and pointed to all the bikes and a sign at the end of them. I took a step back and noticed all the bikes were there to rent. Being so entranced by the beauty of the bikes I had failed to see the shop behind them was renting them out.

'So I can rent this bike now?' I said, wide eyed.

'You have passport?' She leaned her head towards me. I could tell by her inquisitive stare that if I said no I wouldn't be going for a ride on this bike.

'Sure do,' I said, and I pulled out my passport. I dropped it on the ground and almost tripped when I leaned to pick it up. I tried to act straight but there was no point; she just stood there smiling, knowing I was an easy sale.

She took my passport and photocopied it.

'Be careful, full of petrol.' These were her only words of advice as she handed me the keys and two helmets. I stuffed my head in a helmet that was one size too small as she connected the other one to the back of the bike. The helmet was the kind that didn't cover the face, but I was still instantly boiling from the Thailand heat. I flicked my right leg over the seat then lowered myself and kicked up the stand, readying myself for an adventure. I fumbled with the keys until she grabbed them from me.

Ah, she knows I'm drunk, she's kicking me off, I thought.

'It go here,' she said, sticking the key in the ignition and starting the bike. I had a smile the length of my face. I twisted my grip and gave two revs of the ignition, nodded my head at the lady and took off, riding.

Within five minutes of coming into contact with her I was sitting on my new bike. As I began flying around the chaotic streets my face started to hurt a little from my huge grin. I felt a little tug around my neck as my new tie flapped in the wind. I was a drunken, free as a bird disaster waiting to happen.

My decision to hire the bike shaped my whole life. I often wonder if the monk back at the temple knew this. If I hadn't jumped on the bike that day it's possible I might now be dead or in gaol.

Because of the monk I had been enticed to journey up those large stairs. This had left me tired and thirsty when I reached the bottom and the thirst forced me to sit at the bar, where I had a few drinks before noticing the bikes. If I hadn't gone up those stairs the decision to hire the bike, which ended up shaping my life, wouldn't have happened.

The bike wasn't doing too well. I heard spluttering from under me as the engine struggled. I slowed down before coming to a complete stop. After what felt like just a few streets the bike had run out of petrol.

Be careful, full of petrol. I recalled her words. Not five minutes on the bike and I had already been ripped off by the fat lady I had hired it from. I hopped off and looked in every direction. I heard a driver scream out of his open window as his car flew within centimetres of hitting me. I spotted a petrol station that looked maybe 100 metres away. Pushing that distance was hard enough work when sober, never mind drunk and in the Thailand heat.

I bent down, held the handlebars with my left hand and gripped the seat with my right as I started pushing. The heavy bike was deviating off course and strayed closer to the road before a horn and slight screeching of tires reminded me to pull it back into line. Halfway to the station I was spent. I bent down further and rested my head on the smelly seat and closed my eyes. The fumes from passing cars' exhausts almost sent me to sleep.

Beep! Another loud horn took me out of my little rest so I began the remainder of the journey. I pushed a few more metres but had to stop to be sick, probably from fatigue but also a result of the previous twelve hours of consumption. I reached the petrol station and pushed the bike up a short driveway that felt like Mount Everest.

I glanced around the petrol station as I filled the tank. Pollution from the road clouded my already foggy vision. I found myself having another moment like the one I'd had back at the steps. This overbearing feeling of disappointment coursed through me. I had turned my life around and was making people proud. I was going to be in the navy and a champion boxer.

What am I doing here? I thought.

'Fuck, you can be so stupid!' I said to myself as another man filling his tank looked up at me strangely. 'No, no, I'm not talking to you,' I mumbled. My thoughts were running wild and my mind drifted back to the monk again.

Ding. Just ... *Ding.* Be ... *Ding.* Silent ...

I could almost hear the Tibetan bowls being tapped and I felt a slight tingling sensation through my body. I remembered the little monk at the top of the stairs and felt the brewing anger inside me wash away. I tried to focus on the calm feeling I'd had back there. My thoughts slowed and I exhaled.

After thinking about the possibility of a quiet mind, my future seemed bright again.

'When I get back no more drugs or drinking,' I said to myself as the petrol filled the tank. I was going to look for happiness somewhere else.

But that idea was at the heart of my problem: always thinking that happiness was waiting for me somewhere else, somewhere down the line as opposed to right now in the present.

If I was always looking forward for something to be happy about down the line or recalling a past event that was fun was I ever really living at all? Everything was just based on a memory of projection; neither was reality or truth. You can't live your life in the fantasies found in your head and expect happiness. I had to start just being. But what about this spiritual quest I wanted to go on? Wasn't that the same as projecting? My answers would come later.

When I arrived back at the hotel I noticed a big Western-looking biker type on a Harley-Davidson motorbike. He had long blond hair tied in a ponytail and a matching-colour moustache that gave him the typical hard-arsed biker look. I spoke with him about his bike and soon realised by his accent that he was American.

'Yeah, I sell Harleys here in Thailand,' he said, proudly.

'I'm looking to buy a Harley, actually.' *This should get him to let me ride his bike,* I thought to myself. I often lied a lot when drunk to get some kind of advantage. Normally it was to try to impress a female, where I would make out I had more money than I did.

Sometimes it worked, other times not so, and if I was too drunk I would get caught out.

'Can I try yours out?' I motioned getting on his bike.

I don't know if he could smell the alcohol on me or just captured my bullshit, but he didn't give me the chance.

'Get off, you fucking asshole!' he snapped, pushing me aside.

I laughed as I stumbled off. At least I gave it a shot. I entered my hotel room, hot and sweaty from my adventure and dying for a rum. It had been a while since my last drink and sobering up wasn't an option.

'Where the hell you been?' Ruben said, entering the room.

'Everywhere. I went to this amazing temple and . . .' I stopped my tale short. I didn't want to tell him about my brush with the monk. I was halfway through the sentence when my mind, after worrying about what other people thought for so long, jumped in from behind the words to stop me. It didn't want me to be laughed at. It was like my worrying mind reached out from within and slammed my mouth shut. I didn't even have to think about what I was trying to avoid: my mind knew I hated being laughed at so it automatically shut me up.

'I hired a bike and got two helmets. Let's go for a ride!' I downed my drink.

'Fuck that! I'm not getting on the back with you riding. Let's go to a strip bar!' Ruben said.

'Sweet, I'll ride.' I stood and grabbed my helmet, and handed the other to Ruben.

'No. We are walking.' He threw the helmet on the bed.

After arguing for a while we negotiated on getting a taxi. We rode in the back tray of the pickup truck, seats running the length of each side and the ceiling with small fluorescent lights scattered across it. For easy access and to enable passengers to jump in and out, there was no back gate. Cars and scooters lined up behind us could see straight in as Ruben and I chatted away.

'I'll give these guys something to look at!' I hung my bare backside out for people to see.

'Pull up, bro, you can't do that shit here!' he said, tugging at my shirt.

I pulled my pants up and sat quietly.

My contrasting life . . . When straight all I did was worry about people's opinions of me. If drunk, though, I'd have ruthless moments when I couldn't care less – until I sobered up and remembered. I suppose that showing off is another form of worrying what people think. I would try to get as many laughs as possible by doing dumb shit, hoping people would think differently about me. I always liked leaving an impression. My self-worth was low and my insecurities high, so being different at least allowed me to feel special compared with anyone else. Even if that different was embarrassing.

As we approached the club Ruben rang the bell to signal the driver to stop. We stumbled out of the back tray and noticed ladies in skimpy underwear everywhere. 'Hey, sexy man, come here.' They were trying to convince us to come inside a club we already had every intention of entering. As we walked inside we saw that a large framed photo of the star attraction, two beautiful local ladies, was rattling against the wall as the loud thumping bass screamed from large speakers, shaking the whole building. It looked like we had walked into a stadium, the seats lining the walls in rows all facing a particular section.

'What? Look at that!' I yelled.

'What?' Ruben hollered back.

'Look!' I responded, pointing in the direction where all the seats were facing. Two ladies in a half-filled hot tub were putting on a show with each other.

If I were sober I would cringe and feel awkward at strip shows. Once at a friend's party where strippers had been hired I wasn't drinking because I had a fight scheduled a few weeks after it. I sat watching the show as all the boys whistled and tried to grab at the ladies. The strippers caught one of the partygoers filming and stopped the show before snatching his phone. I walked out of the room as I felt incredibly awkward, while everyone else in their intoxicated state hollered and booed that the show had come to an end.

Now I was drunk; now I was doing the whistling.

As the two Thais had sex with each other I looked at the front row and noticed a grey-haired man rubbing his crotch through his pants.

I sat there and watched the show for a couple of minutes but became restless – as you would, being drunk and seeing what I was seeing.

'I'm jumping in!' I said to Ruben, hoping he would be shocked at my suggestion. My ego loved to shock others, as by shocking someone I felt like I surprised them. By surprising someone I felt I knew more than the person, which put me in a position of power. The ego loves power.

'Bullshit, I bet you don't,' Ruben replied with a big grin on his face.

I stood up and pushed my pants down to my ankles before they got tangled around my feet. I had to sit back down to take them off. Ruben laughed, knowing I was going to go through with it. A couple of people from the audience seated behind me saw what I was doing and began cheering. Kicking my underwear free of my feet, I ran and did a belly flop into the hot tub. Bubbles and water splashed everywhere. The singing bowls and Western monk were a distant memory as I was immersed in the sex water.

I put my head above the surface and wiped the bubbles free of my face to the vision of both ladies turning their attention on me.

I was soon a part of the show.

A fat Western man rushed from behind the stage waving his arms and screaming. The loud music didn't allow me to hear what he was saying, but going by his tense face he was pissed off. He came over to the side of the tub and said something to the two girls that wiped the smiles off their faces. The exhibition was brought to an unwanted halt.

The girls climbed out of the tub as the man placed robes around the now delicate-looking ladies and escorted them away. I started dancing on the poles by myself as Ruben took photos. I laugh my arse off even now when I think back to that moment. I still remember Ruben's big grin as he snapped away. I also recall all the men in the crowd telling me to get off and put my clothes back on. I could hear what everyone was saying because, just like the show, the music had stopped.

'Hey, let's go get a massage,' Ruben said, throwing me my shorts.

'Yeah! Perfect!' I keenly replied.

'The massage is the best, I have a big sleep while I'm there. You should have a sleep too, bro, freshen up,' Ruben said, looking out of the corners of his eyes to see my reaction. I sensed that he wanted me to pass out and sober up. Out on the Pattayan street again I could smell cigars being smoked by old men sitting on little stools as music from nearby bars hummed through the area. Nodding my head at the men seated, I tripped.

Ruben laughed.

We came to a nice-looking shop with a small front area encased in shiny wood. Jade green feathered cushions sat on a comfortable-looking lounge that lined the full length of the front of the building. It looked inviting enough for me to jump right on.

'Get up, you dickhead,' Ruben said as he pulled at my arm. I stood back up slowly, and as I looked around I noticed there was no sign of the near-naked ladies enticing a visit.

This was a place for a *proper* massage.

'What are we doing here?' I asked as we entered the shop of disappointment.

'Trust me, it's the best massage ever! Wait until you see out back.' Ruben tried to convince me.

We pushed ahead into the shop, where an old woman waited and welcomed us inside. 'Good evening, gentleman,' the old lady said. 'Please, come in inside.' She led the way, walking through a green curtain that resembled the colour of the cushions on the front lounge.

What we had in front of us soon made me appreciate this place a lot more. I smelled the most beautiful burning oils as slight, soft smoke passed by my face. We were on a balcony looking over water, where two appealing massage tables sat waiting.

This place was beautiful.

Stripping down, Ruben whispered to me, 'Remember, this is a proper massage. No funny business.'

He needn't have worried anyways, because the masseuse wasn't my type. I liked short and petite, but she stood at my height of 190 centimetres.

'Please, sit,' she said in a soft voice that didn't reflect her large frame. First my shoulders were taken to nirvana, and I sat reminiscing on the previous 12 hours. So much had already happened in such a short amount of time. This holiday was already beating out any other I had been on before. While lying down I thought about the monk at the temple.

'We don't *do* meditation, we *are* meditation.'

I could hear his voice. As I heard those words in my head I felt my usual chaotic thoughts quieting. *Am I meditating?* I thought. *You're an idiot; how are you meditating?* My mind butted in to cut me down.

Ding ... ding ... ding ...

With the sounds of the bowls vibrating my aura, Ruben's plan took only a few minutes to work. Between the reminder to just be silent and the incredible massage my thoughts calmed down, and I was out like a light.

I heard whispers and noticed my heavenly massage had stopped. I opened my eyes to see Ruben slowly putting his clothes on.

'What do you think you're doing?' I asked as I wiped the drool from my chin.

'Man! I wanted you to pass out for a while longer,' Ruben said.

'Why?' I asked, wiping my eyes.

'Just so you settle down a bit. I was going to pay the ladies to let you sleep here.'

Not one day into the trip and Ruben had already had enough of drunken Luke.

'Well, that didn't work, did it?' I said jovially, pushing him back onto his massage table.

'You prick,' he laughed as he conceded defeat.

After a short power nap I was feeling fresh. We walked out of the beautiful little cabin and onto the main street, where the sun had started to go down. The dusty, fluorescent bulbs were now the dominant light as they lined the streets. We ducked into a little shop selling alcohol and I bought two Smirnoff blacks, a strong mixed vodka. Ruben looked on sheepishly as he took one from me. I was feeling ecstatic at this point: I was in a foreign country with my brother, and the help from alcohol meant I didn't have a worry in the world.

We sat at a round table in another extremely loud bar, and one of my eyes began to close. This often happened when I was too drunk to see and closing one eye sometimes helped me focus. We faced a stage where a band was playing and a rather short Thai man with purple spikes through his black hair was singing Red Hot Chili Pepper's 'Scar Tissue' in broken English.

I had a moment of reasoning when I lessened the sensations around me; the loudness of the music and the laughs and chatter in the bar had become background noise as I entered my mind to have a chat with myself.

Man, you are pretty buckled, you know you can't fuck up in Thailand. Let's go back to the hotel.

I convinced myself I should go back to the room and sleep. I shook off the common sense as the bar caught my eye, and the loud sounds of the band and crowd returned as I moved a couple of stools to make my access to the bar easier. After a couple more drinks I was unable to stand. Soon I was on my back looking up at Ruben and a lady was laughing. They were trying to help me after I had fallen and pulled a table on top of myself.

I was close to blacking out . . .

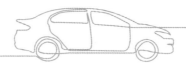

Chapter 5

THE ACCIDENT

Saturday, 22 November

I opened one eye then the other, and closed them both quickly as a bright light stung against the back of my head. I tried to blink repeatedly, but it was tough to adjust to the painful glare.

'Sir,' said a voice I wasn't familiar with.

I attempted to open my eyes again. Everything was still hazy, but slowly I was able to start making things out. Although my eyes had adapted to the light my vision was still cloudy.

Two ladies – one large with red puffy cheeks and unruly black hair and the other a petite beauty – and a man in glasses stood at my side. In the background was a large-screen television playing a show I had never seen before. I was confused. I wasn't on a floor; the surface beneath me was soft. Was I on a bed?

I looked around. Beside me was a machine making the occasional beeping noise and a tube with fluid running through it. I followed the length of the tube and it ran into my arm.

I looked around the room for someone I recognised, hoping to find anyone who could make sense of it all.

'Ruben!' I screamed. The people around the bed began speaking quickly in Thai. 'Where is my brother?' I continued. I began frantically waving my arms and tried to sit up to look behind me. 'Ow!' I screamed in pain. 'My leg!' A hard drumming pain bolted down my right leg. The man in glasses held my chest in an attempt to settle me down.

'What the fuck is happening!?' I pleaded through scared tears.

'Accident, accident,' the tiny beauty announced. The man in glasses tapped her on the shoulder and waved his hand a little, as if asking her to be quiet. Leaning in, he touched my chest. 'Do you know your name, sir?' he asked.

'Luke Kennedy.'

He smiled at the tiny nurse. 'I am Doctor Montri,' he introduced himself, his calm voice and movements giving him a yogi-like presence. 'You were in quite an accident, Luke.' This Thai man's English was better than mine.

Things started falling into place. I wasn't in the bar; I was in a hospital.

'Mr Kennedy, you were riding the motorbike at high speed and collided with a taxi. You are lucky it was a taxi. If it had been a normal car your head would have hit the roof. You had no helmet on. You would have died.' His tone grew more somber as he spoke, hitting me with the seriousness of it all.

I had hit the tray of a pickup truck, and all but one of my injuries were from the waist down. As I lay there with these strangers around me I was panicking. *What is going to happen?* I thought to myself. I had stopped listening.

I was a terrible listener because I was always inside my head. I would normally rely on someone in my company to get the particulars of any information and ask questions later if I needed to. Now I was alone and dazed as if I was an alien experiment that had been abducted, the trio standing and probing at me speaking in a different language. I felt incredibly isolated.

Dr Montri must have noticed the fear in my eyes. He stopped and began speaking quietly to me. 'You broke your tibia and fibula,' he began as he motioned towards my leg. I didn't know what a tibia or fibula was at that point but guessed they were my leg bones.

'We had to put a plate and bolts in your severely broken leg. You had a compound fracture, both bones pierced the skin, so it was a big job.'

I looked down past my chest and all I could see was my right leg bandaged from my foot to just past my knee.

'In the operation we had to cut from here,' the doctor said as he gently touched the bottom of my shin, 'to here.' He moved his hand up the length of my shin and stopped at my knee. 'We placed a large plate in to hold everything together.'

I reached down and rubbed my hip and felt a large bump. I winced from the discomfort and, noticing my distress, Dr Montri asked, 'What is wrong?'

I began pulling my blue hospital gown up like a stage curtain to see what the bump was, dreading what it was about to reveal. My eyes watered in anticipation. What I saw nearly made me sick: a large lump was pushing at my skin, attempting to burst through. I felt my face tremble as I panicked.

'What the fuck?' I shrieked. 'What is it?'

'Broken, broken,' the petite nurse blurted out.

I looked straight over to Dr Montri. He stood looking stunned, as though he wasn't sure what to say.

'Mate, what is it?' I begged, snapping him out of his stare as the two nurses stood behind him arguing together.

The doctor switched back to Thai, speaking rapidly and pointing in different directions. He slowed his frantic actions as he turned back to me. 'It looks like you have either a broken or dislocated hip.'

I understood why the doctor had looked so aghast. In all their haste to get my leg patched up they hadn't realised something was also wrong with my hip.

I was petrified when I realised their incompetence. They had just operated on me but apparently had no idea what they were doing. What kind of hospital was this?

I was pushed down to another room. The hospital was chaotic: loud beeping machines going off, nurses rushing around with clipboards under their arms, patients calling out in discomfort and babies crying.

I wanted to be pushed all the way home.

My bed glided across the titled floor before they turned me into the X-ray room. Entering the quiet room extinguished the chaos outside, and I was introduced to the discomfort of being put under the X-ray machine. It was unbearable. Trying to move around while keeping other parts of my body still was almost impossible. The language barrier was also proving to be tough.

'Turn body left,' the large nurse with the mop of black hair ordered. 'No, wrong, go this way,' she said as she pulled me aggressively to the right. I guess her left was different to mine. After half an hour of what felt like a ransom negotiation we were done X-raying. The nurse's patience had obviously worn thin as she rolled her eyes and stood up. 'Have good day,' she said as she exited the room.

Back in my hospital room, which resembled a hotel with its plasma television and shiny wooden bedside table, I was back to being comfortable thanks to my new best friend – morphine.

* * *

'Luke, it's worse than we thought.' Dr Montri placed my X-rays under a light so I could see. 'You've crushed your hip and pelvis,' he said as he pointed to sections of the X-ray. While I was interested in what was wrong with me my devastation made me near deaf to anything he had to say. I had little trust in their ability to know exactly what was wrong. I envisioned my life turning back to rubbish after fighting so hard to pull myself together. This, I thought, would demolish my efforts and take me back to my turbulent past.

'We need to operate again. A plate needs to be put in to put your hip back together.'

After giving me the news Dr Montri left the room. I was alone, lying there hoping for Ruben to find me soon. *Where was he?* I was terrified. I had been stabbed before and close to death numerous other times, but that moment while lying hopelessly in that bed was the most scared I had been in my whole life.

By myself in a foreign country without any idea what was going on, I felt incredibly sorry for myself. I stared at the ceiling, tears welling up in my eyes. *Why me?* I thought. *Why did I come to Thailand? It's not Thailand's fault! I've acted like a fucking idiot on this trip! Those people in the street I annoyed, the African lady who stormed out of the room, the passengers on the plane starting their trip off anxious because of me. Ruben just wanted to take me away for a good time. What have I done! Please . . . I just want to go home. Mum and Dad are going to be crushed.* I felt a tear slowly run down my cheek.

I'd worked so hard to get my body and mind away from the drama of my past. I had turned it all around and finally had my family proud of me. I had reduced their and my own worries.

I wiped the tears clear as Dr Montri came back in with a whole crew of people, two tall men and three short ladies. This crew looked like they meant business. As I was being pushed down to the operating theatre I looked up at the lights passing by, counting them to try to keep my mind off things. I reached 26 before we entered an elevator. If you think being in an elevator with other people is awkward, try it with a gang who can't understand you and are about to cut you open. If it felt like I was an outer space experiment before it felt even more so now.

I was in a crowded room with people everywhere doing all sorts of things: a man in front of me was pulling slicing utensils out of plastic as the light reflected off the sharp blades, and another man to my right was washing his hands. Two ladies to my left were standing by a machine looking like they were arguing about its function. Nobody was speaking English.

Nobody was comforting me. Nobody, it seemed, *cared*.

I thought back to when I was a five-year-old boy running around the backyard. I tripped and fell over an opening in a water drain and screamed in pain. Mum stopped what she was doing in the kitchen and came out to see what I was crying about. She walked over to me calmly and knelt down as I held my slightly bleeding knee.

She didn't say anything as she cupped my knee in both hands. She blew a soft breath of air before kissing it. She raised her eyes to meet my watery ones. 'Better?' she asked.

'Yep, heaps,' I smiled back.

I wished Mum was there with me. I wanted her caring touch. I blinked.

Suddenly I was doing the same routine from what felt like just moments ago, trying to get the world back into focus. I was returning from a forced sleep again, and instead of the operating theatre I was back in the odd hospital/hotel room.

I scratched at a dull ache in my jaw only to discover a bandage on my chin, apparently another piece of damage from the crash.

These guys didn't realise I had a broken hip. No way I'm letting them fuck with anything on my head, I thought. A clicking in my jaw every time my mouth moved was still not enough to warrant a complaint.

'Success!' Dr Montri said as he entered the room. 'The operation went perfectly well and now all we have to do is recover.'

'How long will I be here?' I really wanted to be at home, even if home meant Sydney's Royal Prince Alfred hospital.

'At least two weeks recovery,' he explained. The hospital was private, so I thought to myself that these guys would want me there as long as possible. Even though I wouldn't be paying for it, the longer I stayed the more cash they received through my insurance. I always thought everyone was out to do the wrong thing when it came to money.

'Luke, they're all fucking conmen. Anyone who's a salesman or asking for some sort of money is trying to do you over. The whole world is filled with pricks wanting your money. Don't trust anyone,' Dad would advise me.

So why wouldn't the same apply here?

I didn't care, though, as travel insurance would cover my extra two-week morphine holiday in this hotel hospital.

I drifted off into another drugged slumber as Dr Montri left the room.

As I slowly woke I recognised the person seated next to my bed. It was Ruben. The sight of seeing my brother was like God had placed an angel by my side: a very ugly, rough-looking angel. I turned to him and smiled. He was holding his chin in his closed hand as he often did and shook his head with a frown.

'What's wrong?' I asked. Never being one to be openly depressed, I was still smiling.

'You okay?' he asked.

'Yeah, sweet,' I laughed.

And just like that he opened up. 'Man, what the fuck happened? You fucked up!'

'But, man, wasn't it a good night!' I laughed. 'Best night of my life.'

'What happened?' he managed to squeeze out through his laughter.

'Bro, I don't really know. The last thing I remember was being in the pub on the floor. What happened after that?' I asked.

'The last time I saw you –' I stared at him as he told the story – 'you were hammered. You pulled tables down on you after you fell over.' This I remembered.

'We left the bar because we were kicked out and hopped into a taxi. I had a girl with me but you were doing my head in!' He was agitated with my shenanigans. 'You were mumbling bullshit. All I could make out was the word "motorbike", then we rocked up to the hotel,' Ruben continued.

We had arrived back at the hotel car park and he forcefully asked me for the keys to the bike. He leant me against a wall for support as he frisked me in search of the keys. 'Where did you put them?' he asked, as if thinking I would give an honest reply. All he got back were more mumbles.

We had been worried about the disgruntled African lady snitching to the police so we had moved hotels and had separate rooms. Ruben entered my room, which had clothes scattered all around an open suitcase, and began rummaging through my stuff to locate the keys. He couldn't find anything, so he decided to take the two helmets to prevent me from riding.

Smart move – technically.

He left me and went next door to his room. After looking out of his peephole for a few minutes to see whether or not I'd walk past, he happily retired to bed with his girl in the firm belief I was staying put.

'Bro, I woke up the next morning and knocked on your fucking door to wake you for breakfast. I banged for ages, so just thought you were still passed out. I walked past reception and heard "Your friend in hospital" from the lady standing behind the counter.' Thinking they had the wrong person, he shrugged it off and headed out for the morning.

After enjoying his buffet breakfast and a day of shopping, Ruben arrived back at the hotel and was approached by the manager, whose English was a lot better than those at reception. 'Your friend who you arrived with was in a motorbike accident.'

Ruben froze. The realisation flogged him in the face as he stared back at the manager.

'Bullshit, open his door!' Hoping for the slight chance they had got it wrong, he headed for my room and entered it to find an empty bed and also two empty bottles of rum. He sat down, looked around at the mess and put his head down. 'Fuck, it *is* my brother in hospital.'

'Mum's been crying, they're calling here soon,' Ruben announced. Not long after the phone rang.

'Luke, Luke.' It was Dad's deep voice.

Hearing the flustered tone of his voice made me realise how serious a situation I was in. He was largely impatient at the best of times but now he sounded like a horse-race caller: the words couldn't get out of his mouth quickly enough.

'What happened?' he snapped. 'You feeling okay? What's broken?' he asked before I got a chance to answer. 'I'm coming over!' he concluded, as though my silence warranted such a move. He wouldn't let me answer, his worry controlling his tongue.

Such was Dad's presence of protection for his family I envisioned him sitting on a Thai Airways flight and telling the pilot to hurry up. I knew if he was in Thailand with us then everything would be okay. He made shit happen. Rolling my eyes at Ruben I said, 'Dad, we are fine.' I didn't want him to worry.

Mum hopped on the phone next. I could tell she had been sobbing, and who could blame her?

I hung up the phone and Ruben was in a hurry to leave. 'You okay by yourself?'

'I'll be sweet,' I slurred.

After Ruben left I sat dozing in and out of sleep. Waking occasionally, I'd worry about not knowing where I was. My worry doubled each time I remembered my predicament.

Chapter 6

POOR SOUL

Sunday, 23 November

Dr Montri stood by my side, his intelligent face a mask of calm as he pushed his glasses further up the bridge of his nose. 'Luke, your travel insurance company rang and asked if you had been drinking.'

I felt my face drain to a pale white. As though I had been dumped into an icy river, every muscle tensed up and I was frozen with fear. *I'm finished!*

'I wasn't drinking,' I lied.

He stood staring at me with his arms at his side. His eyes screamed 'bullshit' but he didn't say a word for a few seconds. 'We didn't take any drug or alcohol tests at the time of the accident,' he went on to explain with a smirk on his face.

Now I was smirking as the colour to my face returned. As I looked around the room I didn't want to contemplate the possibility of having to pay the bill out of my own pocket.

Fuck, what if I have to pay for this? How much do you reckon? I had two surgeries! I've got my own room too.

My thoughts were bouncing around . . . again.

This place is private, that costs heaps. All this ongoing treatment too. Wonder what they charge? Could I get out of paying anyways? All I'd have to do is be able to get in a wheelchair and pushed out into a taxi. Man, a taxi would be so uncomfortable now. Don't be stupid; you can't go. Actually, it could work. Relax, you don't need to anyways, insurance has got this covered. Once I've recovered I'll get transferred comfortably to the airport then jump on a plane to get home. Imagine having to go through customs like this. Ruben would have to push me around in a wheelchair. I wonder if customs would treat me better if I was in a wheelchair. Would I still have to show my passport? Of course, you idiot.

Hang on: my passport! Where's my passport?

I realised that I hadn't seen my passport since the accident. I had been given a plastic bag filled with the gear I had had with me when I crashed: shorts, wallet and, of course, my tie. But no passport.

'Dr Montri, where's my passport?'

'We had to verify your identity when you arrived here.'

'Okay, can I have it back now?'

'You will receive it when you're healthy to leave and discharged.'

Heaps of foreigners must have escaped here without paying.

I had been in hospital for two nights but it felt like I had been there for 10 years. I heard a discussion going on outside that was getting closer to my room. Two people walked straight past but were called upon by a nurse trailing behind. She spoke her native Thai and gestured over to me. In walked a lady and a man accompanied by the nurse. The lady I recognised, but I couldn't remember where from.

Everything was like a bad dream and the morphine's effects clouded my memory and perspective on reality. The man looked like a Thai Frankenstein: his head was abnormally massive. He stood behind the lady, and as she approached he walked around the room pretending not to listen. The lady's identity firmed up as she got closer: she was the stout lady who had loaned me the motorbike. The word 'awkward' couldn't describe this situation.

She grabbed a bag from Frankenstein and placed it on my bed. 'This for you.' The bag was full of cakes.

I was anxious, knowing exactly why she was there. I had smashed her brand new bike. Her gift, as though she was visiting a sick family member, and her obvious fake smile made me cringe. I didn't know what to do so I began unwrapping one of the treats.

'How are you: you okay?' she asked as Frankenstein listened in.

'Yeah, very sore, very scary.' I was trying hopefully to get some pity and be awarded clemency. I bit into the sponge cake. I watched the television and ate her gift as she stood there waiting for me to say something.

I didn't budge. I didn't want to bring up the obvious; I wanted this nightmare to all go away. She reached into her pocket for what I hoped were more sweets but pulled out a piece of paper. She slowly unfolded the paper while searching my face for an expression. 'Bike can't be fix.' She handed me the paper and I could see Thai words with numbers next to them.

She gestured to each word. 'Engine, tank, body,' she went on. The total at the bottom of the paper worked out to around $7,000 Australian.

'Travel insurance will pay for it, I have full insurance.' I explained confidently that travel insurance would cover all my bills and she was sure to get paid. I wasn't actually sure what travel insurance would cover; I just wanted to buy a little more time.

After the money issue was out of the way she became more relaxed and gestured to Frankenstein. 'Camera,' she said to him. He produced a video camera. I thought she wanted to get footage of me all battered up, but she was showing me something on the screen.

'You on TV.' She pressed 'Play' on the camera and I could see what looked like her family sitting on couches. The footage then turned to a TV in her lounge room playing a news report that showed a whole heap of people standing around and flashing sirens in the background.

It soon became clear what all these people were looking at.

The motorbike lady's TV was running a report on my accident so she had recorded it. It showed me lying on the road and leaning up to look at my leg, which had two bones sticking out of it, and people all around me.

I can't describe the feeling I had of seeing myself in that sorry state. The look on my face was one of a scared, drunken mess.

All I had on was a pair of shorts and a tie. Blood and two white bones were protruding from my right leg.

Poor soul.

It was like I was watching a child of my own, and was disappointed in him for the way his life had turned out. *How many times will this shit have to happen before you learn your lesson?* I thought to myself.

The lady was laughing when she first showed me, but soon stopped after seeing my pensive face. 'We come back tomorrow.' She gestured with her head at Frankenstein to leave.

'Great,' I replied. *Looking forward to it,* I sarcastically thought.

As the day ticked by I was forced to sit there with my thoughts. In good times my mind was hard to control. At that stage I don't know if it was all the drugs but my thoughts were immensely dark and frightening. Real life was blending in and out of my nightmares and I couldn't tell the difference.

I woke to a cough, the sort of fake cough that meant someone was attempting to wake me or get my attention.

Ruben had come back wearing a new shirt and carrying bags full of clothes. 'How was your day?' he said as he sat down.

'Bro, the lady whose bike I crashed came in!'

'Fuck! How was that?'

'Awkward! She had paper with how much the bike was worth. About seven thousand Aussie. You reckon insurance will cover it?' I asked.

'Yeah, for sure. If not we might have to take off without paying anything,' Ruben responded.

'Bro, I don't wanna do that shit. Besides, they have my passport.'

'Who: the bike lady?' Ruben sounded worried.

'No, the hospital.'

'All good then, insurance will definitely cover the hospital.'

'Great.' I tried to smile. 'What did you get up to today?' I asked, wanting to hear about a life away from my current trapped state in the hospital.

'Just went shopping and hooked up with a couple of friends from my last trip here,' he went on, but instead of making me feel better his company left me feeling jealous. He was out having a ball and enjoying the trip while I was stuck here.

'Bro, just go,' I said rudely, now feeling pretty pissed off at him.

'What do you fucking mean?' he returned aggressively. 'Why you dirty on me? I got you some shirts and . . .' A noise at the door stopped him.

We both sat silently as a little lady in a wheelchair was pushed into my room by a nurse. 'You hurt me!' she shouted.

'What?' I asked. I'd heard her, but I wanted to make sense of it.

'You hurt me, your bike hit me and I'm hurt.'

Oh, God, please be another morphine-induced dream. 'When you smash your bike flew and hit my leg.'

Please wake up, please wake up, I hoped.

This wasn't a dream; it was a nightmare.

I glanced over at Ruben, feeling sunken, but he stared back at me with a sceptical look and turned to eye up the woman in the chair. With that, she jumped out of her wheelchair and began to walk around the bed with no obvious signs of injury.

'What? There's nothing wrong with you, you're fine!' I fired at her.

She sat back in her wheelchair and pulled the bandage up that covered her knee. 'Big cut, I work in water so I cannot work for months,' she defended.

Dad's right: there're pricks everywhere looking to get money!

Admittedly there was a gash on her leg, but I've had bigger cuts on my face after shaving. I could smell a con but how could I prove anything?

'Okay, travel insurance will cover this, everything will be fine.' She looked at me as though she didn't understand a single word I had said.

'You get money from Australia government.' Her smile explained that she now understood.

I looked over to Ruben as she left the room.

'Fuck that lying bitch,' Ruben shot out.

'Bro, I don't know what to do. Speak to the consulate again.'

'What do you want me to ask?' Ruben said.

'Just tell them what happened,' I explained.

'Fuck this holiday, I'm sick of this shit,' Ruben said as he picked up my bedside phone. We had both been in touch with the Australian consulate, but the idea of speaking to them about this didn't make me feel any better.

'They asked if we had any witnesses to say it didn't happen,' Ruben said while holding the phone to his ear.

I waved my hand in the air in frustration. 'Of course we don't.' I was betting on insurance to cover everything.

'They said they will get back to us. I'm going out,' Ruben said, hanging up the phone and exiting the room.

I was happy he was gone. His bad attitude was depressing me more and now I could just relax a little.

Chapter 7

NO INSURANCE

Monday, 24 November

I woke up after another crappy sleep to see Ruben checking in on me again, and I had to apologise.

'Bro, I'm sorry for yesterday. I don't want to fight.'

'Me neither, I was just pissed off.'

'Man, I really have to go toilet,' I complained.

'I'll get the nurse to get your bedpan.' He started to leave the room.

It was under my bed and Ruben knew this, but there was no way he would pick that up for me.

'Nah, man, my stomach is killing me. I need to go number two.'

It was day three in the hospital and I hadn't yet been able to go due to all the morphine and other painkillers. It had been at least four days since I had gone and in that time I had consumed two bottles of rum mixed with coke, more than 16 Hennessy and lemonades, McDonald's, a kebab, all you can eat buffet and plenty of other food and drink. My stomach was giving me a lot of grief and I was sure it wasn't going to be good.

'What do you want me to do?' Ruben scoffed with a smile.

'Call the nurses, ask them,' I replied, laughing myself and happy to see him smiling.

I had stood up to use the toilet a couple of times with crutches and assisted by the nurses, but that was only to pee. There was no chance I could sit down on a toilet seat with my injuries.

Two nurses came in and I explained my situation. They left and returned with a white, tarp-like sheet they unfolded. 'Go on this.'

'What do you mean?' I gasped.

'We lay it under you and you just go.'

My thoughts ran away as I could picture the entire bed filling up then pouring over the side. My bad leg was elevated in a sling and the two nurses lifted my left leg so it was also elevated. Ruben just sat there next to me and I felt incredibly embarrassed. Each nurse grabbed an end of the tarp and stood on opposite sides at the base of the bed. The nurse on my right nodded her head, and in unison they ran the tarp half the length of my bed with my legs dangling above. They tucked it under my back then stood to the side, gazing at my bare bum.

'Go,' one nurse said with a wave of her arm.

'What: just go?' I asked.

'Yes,' she replied, frustrated.

Feeling complete relief mixed with massive disgust, I pushed . . . and kept pushing. The noises were terrible. I looked at the nurses and caught them glaring at each other with a look that said: *you have got to be fucking kidding me*.

It just kept going.

'Bro,' Ruben said through a laugh, his hand covering his mouth as he pinched his nose.

To their credit the nurses took it all in their stride and got on with the job. They picked up the now very heavy tarp and placed it in a large mobile garbage bin before cleaning me. I was feeling a lot better so Ruben left for the day, shaking his head and still laughing as he walked out the door.

I went through another day filled with nightmares. I woke out of a hellish dream that featured me getting hit by a car and then it reversing over me.

A tall, slim nurse walked into the room and noticed my distressed look. 'You okay?' she asked.

'Yeah, I'm fine,' I lied.

'You look scared,' she responded.

'Just having some bad dreams, that's all.' I attempted to lighten the situation. Inside, though, my body was tense, my breaths shortening by the hour. My chest was thumping down with each breath as if it was going to cave in. My stomach bubbled in pain as though I had swallowed acid. The blood running through my veins felt electric as the anxiety threatened to explode through my skin.

'You need to take your mind somewhere peaceful,' she said, standing closer to my bed.

'How can I?' I rudely said back.

'Listen to the music being played,' she said softly, her eyes shifting sideways as though she was trying to hear something.

'I don't have any music,' I said.

'You can't hear the music?' She was looking a little concerned.

'No, I don't have any!' I answered again, slightly annoyed at having to do so.

'I mean, you can't hear the music being played, the piano?' she asked, now seeming to be worried.

'What are you talking about, what piano?' I was intrigued. My thoughts were frantic at this point and I had no idea what was going on.

'Every day an old lady comes and plays the piano for four hours for patients to have peace. She is playing now. You can't hear?' she said. To increase my chances of hearing she then held her breath.

'I can't hear anything.' I thought she was playing games. Then I got a little worried, thinking I was going deaf.

She put both her hands on my chest, implying for me to be still. 'Just breathe,' she insisted before closing her eyes. I took a deep breath in and that alone settled me. It was like a soft heavenly angel had flown into my lungs and spread its wings, allowing me to breathe air filled with life. I felt weightless.

The tension in my body was gone as I continued breathing. Slowly, I heard a soft tone, the sounds of a sparkling piano being played. The smooth magic entered my ears, its energy washing away any negative thoughts. With my eyes closed I pictured the old lady with her aged but soothing face, her eyes dimmed slightly to show her deep love. Sitting on a cloud, her fingers were being caressed by the white keys, the piano moving her fingers rather than the other way around. The piano, it seemed, was alive. Each note was being played in slow motion. With the touch of each key I was sent further into relaxation. My body tingled as the music became a part of me. I was floating.

'Be silent to hear the beauty,' I heard from the nurse as her hands left my chest and she exited the room. I kept my eyes closed, smiling to myself. I soon fell into a deep, dreamless sleep.

The soulful power of music. I now relish listening to music, often listening to chillstep while a teacher drops deep lessons to me.

While listening the softening tones of music calm your body, ease tension and smooth out your stickiness. The music opens your pores, ears and mind, readying your soul. The volume then lowers a touch as your body marinates in the loving frequency, now tender enough to receive the magic. With a presence strong enough for no doubt or worry to penetrate the questioning mind is now silent, the words dancing out of the teacher's mouth and gliding through every open crevice of your being. Like a stream of water meeting a rock face the words manoeuvre around the mind, knowing that the mind doesn't understand but the soul does, so the stream continues towards its resting place.

With the words reaching and touching the very depths of your essence, the stream reaches the cliff face and sits at the top of its final fall, and it's then the right moment to solidify the teaching. With a split second of silence, a gap long enough to feel the stillness, a trusting tension stops your breath and then it comes . . . The stream is now a waterfall as the raised volume of a deep beat hugs the words into your heart, taking your breath away, closing even your eyes to stop any of it leaving you and now that lesson is yours.

'Bro.' I was woken abruptly by Ruben.

Going by sharpness in his voice and his widened eyes, I could tell something was very wrong.

'What now?' I asked.

'Man, I've got some bullshit news.' He stood looking at me as though he were trying to build up some suspense. I knew what he was doing.

Whenever I found out about news and was about to tell someone who didn't know my ego would exude excitement. Even if it was bad news my ego would be aroused. I'd feel superior to the person who didn't yet know the information.

Guess what?

This was a common question I would ask to build that mystery and maintain a hold on the other person. My mind wanted to hold on to the moment when I knew more than them, even just a little while. I would often catch myself ringing people to inform them of some news I'd heard, getting off on the fact that I was the one to tell them.

Always being in my head, I just wanted my ego stimulated. I wanted to feel like I knew more. It was incredibly selfish of me. The reality was that all I cared about was my false mind-made power rather than the actual bad news I was telling someone. I now often observe others doing it, and it makes me feel sick knowing I used to be the same. It's similar to when someone was telling a story and I would only listen slightly, just enough to go inside my head to think of a story that would outdo theirs.

'Yeah, you think that's bad, well, you should have seen what happened to me ...'

Playing the victim, the poor me, is another one of the ego's many tools. When living through victimhood people try to outdo each other with how shitty their lives are. 'You think your life is bad, look at mine!'

'Ah, that's nothing. Guess what happened to me?'

'That's not doing it tough, you've got more money than me.'

'Yeah, I had four people I know die last year.'

'My upbringing was worse than that.'

'My health is terrible, I take more pills than you!'

And on and on it goes.

Victim mentality is the easiest for the ego to fall into because it doesn't have to do anything besides feel bad. The mind loves stimulating worry and victimisation, which creates separation, and to the ego separation means different. Different equals unique. The ego loves uniqueness.

People aren't even aware they're doing these things, and that's the issue.

Ruben was doing exactly that here, telling me he had some bad news and then not revealing it to make me beg.

'Well, what is it?' I asked angrily.

'Man,' he said, still delaying the reveal.

'What?' I roared.

'Travel insurance isn't going to cover you.'

Travel insurance isn't going to cover you.

Travel insurance isn't going to cover you.

The words echoed in my head, tormenting me.

I looked at him then looked away, fully appreciating the service I had been getting in this hotel/hospital room. I would now have to pay for it all.

The phone rang.

'Luke, Luke.' It was Dad again, doing that thing where he repeated my name whenever we got on the phone. 'Have you spoken to your brother? Travel insurance isn't going to cover you.'

Travel insurance isn't going to cover you.

There was the echo again of those seven words. When said one by one they didn't mean much, but when put together it amounted to absolute disaster.

'Dad, they *have* to cover me. The doctors didn't take a blood test so they can't prove I had been drinking.' I held high hopes.

'Mate, it's because you were on a motorbike. Travel insurance doesn't cover such accidents,' he replied as though repeating the exact words he just heard from someone who had informed him.

'Ruben got us full insurance, it *has* to cover us,' I alleged, hoping to be correct.

I later learned that for travel insurance to cover motorbikes you need to get an actual riding licence in Thailand. I do know that it wouldn't have stopped me from getting a bike anyway.

'You have to find out how much the hospital bill is up to. We have to get you out of there.' Dad's voice was intense.

I hung up the phone and turned back to Ruben as the situation registered slowly.

What if it's a few thousand dollars? We can't afford that. I will have to try to escape.

How can I with this leg! I will be thrown in gaol.

My mind began with its harsh scenarios as it always did.

Fuck, imagine being in a Thai gaol. What if the Thai Frankenstein wants to get me? How can I fight like this? If I stood up to fight my leg would crumble. Imagine getting tackled by Frankenstein in this state.

The thought of getting tackled to the ground sent a chilling pain up my leg.

'Go see what the bill is so far,' I said to Ruben, who left in a hurry to fetch the information. I sat there alone.

'Fuck, is this real?' I whispered to myself. There was a lump in my throat, and I felt as though I might start crying. I would have to pay for this hospital stay.

Fuck, the motorbike! Like a sudden bolt of thunder through my entire being I remembered the brand new bike I would have to pay for. Could this get any worse?

'Oh, no, the injured lady,' I said through a defeated sigh. *Does that mean I have to pay compensation for the lady with the paper cut on her knee?* I thought. Everything kept adding up.

The room closed in on me; even the morphine couldn't stop my panic attack. The more my mind reeled the more my body tensed up. It got harder to catch my breath and my vision closed in on me.

I began thinking of my navy career to try to cheer myself up. I told myself that the money I earned from being in the navy would cover this and hoping of course they would still accept me with these injuries. *Of course they will. Maybe not.*

Ruben returned with a piece of paper and a look on his face that implied things were about to get worse.

'What's the damage?' I said casually, hoping for a positive reply.

'Eighteen thousand, eight hundred,' he said.

'Thank God, just shy of six hundred dollars, sweet,' I responded. Ruben's face sank. 'Not sweet, mate, it's eighteen thousand, eight hundred *Australian* dollars.' He tossed the paper on my chest, and it felt like a brick.

If I was standing I would have fainted. The past half an hour had me spinning. Each word spoken, it seemed, was trying to outdo the previous one by pissing me off more. I wished for it to be another bad dream. I looked at the paper and saw it was an itemised receipt. They had charged me as if I had bought each individual instrument they used in the operation.

What can we do? I thought. The phone rang again and I knew it would be Dad. 'You answer it,' I said to Ruben.

He picked up the phone and I could hear Dad's muffled voice on the line. 'Eighteen thousand, eight hundred *Australian* dollars.' Ruben emphasised the word 'Australian' so Dad didn't make the same mistake I had. I couldn't hear anything on the other line for a few seconds, then he spoke. Ruben passed me the phone.

'You have to get out of there. We will try to come up with the money but you've got to get yourself organised and get the fuck out of that joint now. It's costing too much every second you're there,' Dad said.

He hung up and I turned to Ruben.

'Fuck them. Order a taxi and we will just leave early in the morning.' I hoped for a possible escape without paying.

'They have your passport.' He extinguished my wide-eyed suggestion.

As day turned into night I sat alone compounding my bad thoughts. Okay, the bill is probably at $20,000 after tonight's stay, plus the bike $7,000 and the injured lady seeking compensation for God knows how much.

What are we going to do?

'How much cash we got left?' I asked Ruben.

'About one and a half thousand Aussie.'

'That's it? What happened to it all?' I asked, suspiciously.

'What? Don't think I fucking spent it.'

'I got eight thousand in Sydney!' I responded.

'Our flights took nearly half of that, then accommodation and partying over the last two days. I got us some good clothes. It just goes, bro!'

'Yeah, fair enough. But fuck, what are we going to do?'

'Gunna have to call Mum and Dad,' Ruben said, knowing that no matter what they would be there for us.

'Yeah, they've got no cash, though, but Dad will get it off someone. Find out how much we need on top of our fifteen hundred.'

'We need that fifteen hundred just to get by while we're over here! I've gotta eat and still do stuff,' Ruben said.

'Yeah, true. So Dad will have to come up with all the money.'

Mum and Dad lived from pay cheque to pay cheque. *What have I done to them?* I thought.

I couldn't control my anger towards myself. I pictured Mum in our green fibro Housing Commission home sitting down crying. Dad would no doubt be out and about seeing some friends to try to come up with more than $20,000. Dad was a proud man and hated borrowing money from people.

I hated myself at this point.

Even though it was my fault I was also angry at Ruben, thinking he should have known about travel insurance not covering the bikes. At least blaming him took some of the tension away from me.

Chapter 8

LIARS

Tuesday, 25 November

On Tuesday morning, day four after the accident, I lay alone after a night with zero sleep. I dreaded anybody coming into the room, and each time somebody did I expected them to tell me I owed them something too.

I flicked the television on to take my thoughts off things. The news was on. The reporter spoke in Thai and in the background was a lounge room with upturned furniture and what looked like blood smeared across the walls. I read some of the subtitles and made out a story about a local mob that had raided the house and killed someone over money. I felt sick and in a little shock as the cameraman zoomed to the right of the reporter to show the victim still lying there. I flicked the news off and stared at the ceiling, my heart racing.

I looked over at the doorway and saw Ruben entering the room looking dead tired.

'Dad got over twenty grand.' The words fell out of his mouth as he sat down. Dad was miraculously able to get a $21,000 loan from a bank. Relief came over me at the same time as pity. I was really sorry my parents had to go through this, knowing full well how that kind of money would have helped back home. They would do anything for us. Getting me out of a foreign country in the condition I was in would have been the only thing on their minds.

Ruben called for Dr Montri.

'We are leaving tonight at roughly two am to get a five-thirty am flight home,' Ruben informed him.

'Impossible, it's impossible for you to leave.'

I looked at Ruben, and for a split second I felt like I was being held captive.

'You will be in too much pain, very uncomfortable on the plane. You have to be here for at least another week,' Dr Montri went on. 'The risk of infection if you aren't in hospital is huge. Infection could mean amputation.'

My panic about being held captive disappeared and was replaced with worry about losing my leg.

'Mate, I'll be fine. Just drug me up and I'll be okay.' Thinking about the two-hour taxi ride then the flight home, racing against the clock of infection, seemed like a marathon effort.

After a long discussion about us leaving he agreed to let us go and told me he would give me some very strong painkillers.

'Sweet, we can get out of here,' I said to Ruben as Dr Montri left the room. 'Bro, the motorbike and injured ladies will be back today at one to organise their coin.'

We had promised the bike owner and the supposedly injured lady that if they came just after lunchtime we would have the details regarding our travel insurance and their payments. This was not a lie, because at the time we promised this we firmly believed we were fully insured and would be covered.

But things had changed since then.

The only way out was to get Dad to try to get an extra $7,000 for the bike, then we still had the injured lady to deal with. It was impossible. We wouldn't be able to get any more money, or we could tell them we didn't have the money and face possible gaol time and get strangled by the bike lady's Frankenstein friend.

Then I had an idea.

'Ruben, when they all come in leave the room, go to a pay phone and call the hospital and get put through to my room,' I said.

'What the hell for?' he asked as I sat in deep thought.

'When they get here leave the room.' I stopped to think a little more. 'Call the hospital and pretend you're from the Australian consulate, and tell them they have nothing to worry about, that they'll get their money.'

'No fucking way. I'm not doing that shit. It's not right.'

'I want them to get their money, bro, but we haven't got anything. We're finished. We can't give them anything,' I said, defeated.

'We've gotta somehow get some money, we can't do that to them. They struggle bad over here,' Ruben responded.

'We can't. We have no money here or back home. They might get us sent to gaol. Just do it.'

It won't work anyways,' he said.

'It will, man, we have no choice,' I pleaded.

'Let's leave before they get here,' Ruben said, excited as though coming up with a bright idea.

'They have my passport and won't give it back until the money gets wired through, which is after the time they are due here.'

'I'm still not doing it.'

'You have to!' I begged.

'It won't work.'

'It might!' I pleaded, feeling defeated. Every word of the argument was draining my dwindling supply of energy.

He sat down, and I could see him living the experience in his mind. He frowned, shrugged his shoulders and shook his head, accepting it was our only option.

'Sweet,' I said, as he continued to shake his head slowly with his hand over his mouth.

It was by then 12.45 pm, 15 minutes before they were due. I could hear a number of people coming up the hallway.

I'd be early too for $7,000.

Ruben sat up in his chair and tugged at the bottom of his crinkled shirt, trying to look sharp. It was the motorbike lady with her good friend Frankenstein and one nurse. Bike lady looked a lot happier this time than she had during the first visit, and who could blame her? Not 30 seconds later the injured wheelchair lady was pushed into the room by two men. My room was packed with people expecting great news. I wasn't going to disappoint.

'I spoke to the Australian consulate and you are all going to get reimbursed,' I announced as Ruben gracefully exited the room. They were looking at each other with confused looks on their faces. 'Oh, sorry, I mean you will all get paid money,' I explained further.

'How much?' one of the men with the wheelchair lady said in an instant.

'I don't know how much she is getting, but the consulate said they will sort everything out,' I said.

He started speaking in Thai to the man with him and the wheelchair lady, who sat bent necked to look up at them.

'Where are they? How do we get our money?' the same man asked.

'They told me they would call at one when you are all here to arrange a meeting for you to get your money. All you have to do is speak to them and you will get your money.' I repeated the words 'get your money' in the hope it would get in their minds somehow and they would accept they would be paid.

A couple of minutes passed that felt like an hour. The room was full of Thai chatter.

I pictured Ruben picking up a pay phone and pushing a few numbers before hanging up, doubting the situation. I could picture him arguing with himself.

Come on, I thought.

Ring ring ring ring.

Game time.

'Hello.' I tried to act upbeat and smiled to the crowd of onlookers.

'Bro, this isn't going to work,' I heard Ruben say.

'I'll just put them on.' I smiled and handed the phone to the lady in the wheelchair. I could hear Ruben still talking as I passed over the phone.

The lady started speaking in Thai to Ruben.

'No, no, no, English, they are Australian, speak English.' Acting as though she represented the bunch, the motorbike lady took the phone and started speaking in broken English.

I sat with a stupid smile on my face and looked on. After 30 seconds of speaking she started smiling too and was nodding her head to the others. Ruben had promised them that if they came to the consulate the next day (by which time we would be into our second movie on the flight) they would get their money. After she spoke to the others they began cheering and laughing. They said 'Goodbye' and left the room.

Ruben came back looking as though he had run a marathon and sat on the couch. 'I can't believe they fell for that shit,' he said. 'I feel like a prick.'

'Shhh,' I tried to quieten him as I looked towards the door.

'Relax, no one is there,' he shot back.

'Thanks, man,' I said.

'I'm over this,' he growled.

'The money will come through from Dad and we will be out of here soon.' I tried to cheer him up.

Dr Montri repeatedly entered my room without any real sign of doing anything. I started thinking that maybe he was on to us and knew we weren't going to pay the others.

'Why you have to leave so quick?' he asked on one of his trips into my room.

'Mate, we can't afford to stay here. That's all the money my dad could come up with.'

'The money has gone through,' he stated, handing me my passport. He nodded at us, a goodbye maybe, and left the room.

'Bro, let's get out of here now.'

'Relax, man, we are sweet. No one is coming back; they all think they're getting paid tomorrow,' he said.

My mind spun up all the worst scenarios imaginable. I could picture them finding out we had lied then come storming into the hospital like a mob with flaming torches, forcing their way into my room and the nurses joining them because we had lied to their people.

'Mate, seriously, let's go!' I demanded.

'We aren't going anywhere until tonight,' he said, half asleep.

I had to wait it out for more than 12 hours, with my crazy thoughts waiting for the mob to return with their torches. As day turned into night the phone rang.

'Luke?' I heard a voice I couldn't mistake.

It was Anne, my ex-girlfriend who I was with for a few years. With a frisson of excitement, her voice had me feeling like I was at home.

I wished I was there with her.

Even though our relationship was over, when I heard her voice I missed her. We talked for over an hour. Even while talking to my loved ones, though, my mind would slip into worry. I could picture Anne's mum in the background telling her to hang up, not only for the massive international phone bill but, unlike us, she knew our relationship wasn't one worth saving. I stopped listening to Anne, only hearing every second word as my mind was elsewhere.

'Luke, are you listening?' Anne knew me well as she attempted to snap me out of my incessant thinking.

She explained that she had moved my belongings from my place to hers. She reasoned that this would be the best for me because my unit had stairs.

'My place will be easier to get around.' Her place had stairs as well, but she was simply trying to justify her actions. In reality she just wanted us back together. Anne still lived at home but her parents had made the bottom of their house into a separate living area and bedroom so it was like Anne's own crib.

It made me feel warm knowing I was going back to Anne's, that she would look after me.

'Anne, my jaw is buckled,' I slurred. After speaking for so long my jaw was getting worse and my speech was beginning to slur. I couldn't wait to get back home and go to the hospital to get everything checked out.

'Okay, babe, I will let you go. I love you so much.' Anne had worked hard to move all of my stuff so we could be together.

I was looking forward to spending time with her again. After our talk Ruben walked in with his suitcase, placed it by his seat and sat down.

'Anne just called. She's moving my stuff to hers so she can look after me.'

'That bitch is crazy!' he exclaimed, and rolled his eyes. He knew our relationship was one that was destined to fall apart.

I guess when you think you love somebody you are blind to most of the negatives and only think of the great times, holding hope for the possibilities rather than realities. You tend to believe what you want to believe and dismiss any other points of view.

Never underestimate the power of denial.

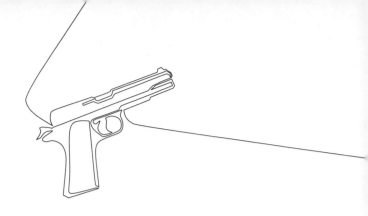

Chapter 9

NOT GOING HOME

Wednesday, 26 November; 2.30 am

It was time for us to leave. I had taken some strong painkillers to help me get through the taxi ride to the airport. I was feeling really groggy, but at least we were going home. We had gotten away with it! We'd be halfway home by the time the people we owed money to would be arriving at the consulate.

Or so we thought.

Two men from the hospital helped me into my wheelchair.

'Get a photo of me with these guys, Ruben.' When I looked at the image I saw total contrast – I had a smile spreading the length of my face and my two thumbs up, and they were both frowning. They gave me a little bag, the kind you get jewellery in, but this was full of drugs. I had enough painkillers on me to kill a rhinoceros.

We got outside and they helped me into the back of a taxi, and I sat leaning on the door with my legs straight across the seat. I looked up expecting a farewell ceremony from the hospital team; all I got was a look at their backs as they walked away.

The drugs had really kicked in and the pain in my leg was all but gone. I felt I was underwater with my eyes open, my vision extremely blurry. At that stage if I didn't have legs I wouldn't have been able to tell. I was flying. Ruben didn't say a word for about an hour. It was as though he had simply had enough of me and couldn't wait to get home.

Couldn't blame him, really.

After a while he asked the obligatory question: 'You okay?' He didn't even look at me.

'Yeah, I'm cool,' I mumbled.

'We will be there in forty-five. Gives us heaps of time to get our flight.' Ruben tried to brighten me up.

I started getting very uncomfortable. After being in bed for so long my body was extra sensitive. My tail bone was rubbing on the seat and becoming quickly irritated. We were 10 minutes away from the airport.

I can do this. Chequered flag in sight . . .

I could picture Dad's face as he picked us up at the other end. I imagined hugging him and feeling safe in his arms.

With that thought I let the weight of the drugs force my head to slump down and I stared at my leg.

'Oh, shit,' Ruben muttered.

I had become so content with the fact that I was on my way home that I didn't want to look up and face what he meant by those two words. The tone of his voice signalled there might be trouble ahead. The taxi slowed as I succumbed to facing reality and looked up. About 50 men stood in the middle of the dark road blocking our path.

As we crept closer I clenched my teeth together in terror. Two men were holding large guns that were strapped to their shoulders like ladies' handbags, and the men standing behind these two were armed with sticks, bricks and machetes. They wore yellow bandanas across their faces to hide their identities. The taxi stopped and the armed men closed in on us and began circling the car.

I'll pay, I'll pay, I thought.

Seven thousand dollars plus the rest was a lot of money in Thailand and these guys were willing to kill us for it, but how did they know we were getting away? Had the doctor given us up? I knew he had been acting strange on the last day and that he was up to something. I didn't want to believe it, though.

We had formed a nice little relationship, but I guess he snitched on us. He did the right thing by his people, but to us at the time it was a disaster.

If I wasn't crippled in the back I would have been proactive about the situation. I might have gotten out swinging punches, or leapt out to hop in the front seat and run them over, or at least jumped out to try to reason with the guys. I could be pretty persuasive in most situations.

I don't know how these guys would have taken to my attempted reasoning. Not being able to do anything I just sat there pretty relaxed, considering I was about to get seriously hurt or killed.

I was resigned to the fact and even slightly appreciated the situation. These guys were about to get their own back after a foreigner tried to do the dirty on them.

Fair is fair.

I felt like a mouse trapped in a glass cage, snakes plaguing the outside and tapping on the glass with their menacing tongues as they slithered closer. These guys were everywhere. The taxi driver wound down his window after one of the men knocked on it with the barrel of his gun.

The gun-wielding man leaned into the window and spoke to the taxi driver, his gun swinging uncontrollably from his shoulder. The language barrier was difficult. At least if it had been in English we would have known what situation we were in.

Going by the armed man's voice it seemed as though he was about to play hide and seek with us, but his tone didn't mirror his appearance. His voice intimated he was a little boy, but it was actually a man in possession of a weapon designed to kill. As the conversation continued the others outside the car stared at me. The taxi driver then said something loudly and gestured in my direction.

The gun man stretched his head further into the car, twisting his neck to look me dead in the eyes.

Time froze.

All I could see were his glassy eyes. They told me the story of struggle; I could tell this man had done it all. Our moment together was breathtaking, and I felt his pain.

Was I about to feel my own?

He continued his deep stare into my eyes, and the whole of Thailand disappeared. There was no taxi, there was no injury, there wasn't even a Luke. All that remained was two souls connecting, each understanding the other's current struggle. Time was erased. A few moments ticked by but it could have been a few lifetimes; I couldn't tell. My breath slowed, as did his. The rhythm of our breaths merged and we were one.

Bang! An explosion far in the distance snapped us out of our oneness and brought our surroundings back into focus. We continued to look at each other but the taxi, my injury, the crowd of people standing around our taxi: everything was back.

'Mate,' I attempted to start with my excuse, trying to tell him I was sorry for ripping off his people.

'Shhh.' He brought his finger to his bandana-covered lips.

As I read his eyes he continued to focus on mine as though trying to do the same. There was no use in trying to come up with an excuse; words weren't needed here. We had already said so much with our eyes.

Our gaze was broken as he suddenly shot a single word from his mouth and gestured to the others. The slithering snakes turned into tamed men, obeying his command and standing aside as we drove slowly through. I looked out of my window and caught his eyes once again. I couldn't look away.

I was in a trance.

I felt for this man. I didn't know what all this was about but I knew whatever it was he was struggling for he believed in it, and he would've killed or been killed for it. I felt his pain. When my mind slowed and we were one I could actually feel his heavy life. It brought out emotion in me that I welcomed. Even though it was sad I enjoyed it.

I found it hard to be empathetic to people or feel emotion. I was too much in my head. Whenever we're in our heads there is no genuine connection. Without connection there's no empathy or emotions to feel. Emotions, empathy, gratitude and real happiness come from beyond thought. If your mind is ticking it's hard to feel these, so when you ease your thoughts your soul expresses.

'What the fuck was that shit?' Ruben said to the driver.

'I don't think you go home,' the driver said.

'What do you mean?' Ruben asked. 'Speed up, then, if you think we will miss the flight!'

'Airport finished, many people at airport, stopping the planes. Protest,' the driver tried to explain.

Ruben turned in his seat to look at me, shaking his head. 'What the fuck? I thought they were from the people we owed the money to,' he said.

'Me too, bro,' I said, exhausted.

'What were you trying to say to him?' Ruben asked.

'Man, I was about to give myself up by apologising for ripping his people off!' I said.

'Fuck, lucky he shut you up.'

Just ... be ... silent ...

Later, when watching the news, I found out it had been a group called the People's Alliance for Democracy (PAD) and they had executed what they called 'Operation Hiroshima'. Hundreds of PAD members dressed in yellow blocked both entrances of the terminal building and blockaded the main road to Suvarnabhumi International Airport in Bangkok. The group that had pulled us up was part of the terminal blockades, and it had been directly after they overpowered hundreds of policemen armed with riot gear.

At 4.30 on the morning of 26 November 2008 three explosions went off on the fourth floor of Suvarnabhumi outside the passenger terminal. We arrived a few minutes after the explosions. Another explosion went off at 6.00 am, this one injuring several people. The PAD did not allow the police or forensics experts to investigate.

The PAD was defiant. Their leader, Suriyasai Katasila, announced they would fight off the police. Was he the man who had told me to shut up?

'If the government wants to clear the protesters let it try. The PAD will protect all locations because we are using our rights to demonstrate peacefully without causing damages to state properties or rioting,' Suriyasai said. He also threatened to use human shields if police attempted to disperse the PAD. Groups of 300 to 400 women were assigned to physically surround each PAD leader. Foreign journalists reported that the PAD was paying people to join them at the airport, with extra payment being given to parents who brought babies and children.

I'm not sure I believed the reporters about the PAD using kids as human shields. I have since decided to make up my own mind on most things, especially because I experienced it and saw how these protesters were really acting.

Police manned checkpoints on roads leading to the airport. At one checkpoint they found 15 home-made guns, an axe and other weapons in a Dharma army six-wheel truck taking 20 protesters to Suvarnabhumi airport. Another checkpoint found an Uzi submachine gun, home-made guns, ammunition, slingshots, bulletproof vests and metal rods. The vehicle had the universally recognised Red Cross signs on its exterior to give the impression it was being used for medical emergencies. At another checkpoint about 2 kilometres from the airport an attack by armed PAD forces in vehicles caused the police to withdraw. Police Senior Sergeant Major Sompop Nathee later returned to the scene of the clash and was detained by PAD forces. He was interrogated by PAD leader Samran Rodphet and then detained inside the airport. Reporters and photographers tried to follow Sompop to his interrogation, but PAD forces wouldn't allow them to.

They were attempting to bring down their prime minister Somchai Wongsawat, who they believed was ruining the country. I couldn't really understand it all. When it comes to politics I keep my distance. Even in Australia, if someone is talking politics I drift off into my own world as I would prefer not to waste my energy on it. They had machine guns, grenades and all sorts of other toys to play with and we were stuck in the middle of it.

Our faded yellow taxi pulled up at the airport in the middle of thousands of pissed off Thais. Ruben put his hand on the door handle, hesitating to open it.

The taxi driver noticed. 'If they wanted to kill you they would have done it back there.' That made sense.

If they let us through in darkness at the armed blockade without any drama, a spot where they easily could have murdered us, then it was likely they would do the same here.

'Good point,' Ruben agreed. He jumped out at the terminal drop-off point, but stuck his head back in to speak to me.

'I'll be back soon. Our flight doesn't leave for an hour anyway,' he said, before darting off into the crowd.

I sat waiting on Ruben's return and was trying to adjust to the massive blinding lights of the airport terminal. We had been taxiing in darkness for a couple of hours so the lights were really hard to get used to. My leg began thumping, its powerful pain a strong contender against the painkillers. I dug through my drug bag for more. I had no water, so I built up some saliva in my mouth. With the minimal fluid the two tablets went down my throat like a fat kid on a dry slippery dip. I sat with the pain, begging for it to go away. The driver was sitting still, happy that the meter was still running.

Ten minutes passed.

Where the hell is he? Hope he's okay, I thought about Ruben.

'Your friend take very long,' the driver said, breaking the silence.

No shit.

'Got one!' I heard screaming from behind the car. Ruben was pushing a wheelchair through all the protesters. My face lit up in a smile. I knew he cared; he looked excited to have been able to help me.

'Man, there's no one to help, no airport workers or anything!' Ruben said, opening my door. It was a relief to be getting out of that enclosed taxi, but the mix between pain and drowsiness from the drugs had my head spinning, I was tripping out.

As he pushed me through the large electric doors we were confronted by a sight I'll never forget. The airport was jam-packed, not only with travellers but with protestors. The chanting and screaming were deafening.

'Hopefully we can still get our flight,' Ruben said. I turned and glanced up at him, thinking he was an absolute idiot.

I looked around at the other travellers and noticed they didn't look too disturbed considering the situation we were all in. My wonders about their relaxed attitude were answered when protesters approached me and apologised, then handed me food.

'We sorry, we know you can't go home, this is only way we are listened to in Thailand. We are very sorry,' a man said as he placed a cake on my lap.

These guys were really apologetic, giving us foreigners' food and bowing as we accepted. Time and again I heard genuine apologies; we even had a group of people explaining why it had to be done.

Ruben pushed me around for what felt like an hour. My judgement of time and space was strangled by the extreme amount of drugs I had consumed. I reached to grab the cake on my lap but missed it and grabbed my knee.

'You alright, bro?' Ruben asked.

'Call Dad, he will know what to do,' I slurred.

Ruben called Dad; we needed some reassurance that we would get home soon. As Ruben spoke he looked around for airline staff, hoping to get some help.

'It doesn't look like we will, the flight was supposed to leave five minutes ago,' I heard Ruben say on the phone.

Fuck, we've missed our flight. My thoughts were sharper than my sloppy speech.

'Yeah, Luke is sweet, he's sitting in his wheelchair.' He continued speaking for a few minutes.

Ruben hung up the phone and I couldn't resist.

'Still think we can make our flight?'

'Get fucked,' he snapped.

Ruben was back on the phone to a consulate official in Australia. He was told to find a lady who was dealing with foreigners on the other side of the airport.

'I'll be back in about fifteen minutes,' he said before disappearing.

'What happened?' a man in his early 20s asked as he walked over to me. He stood over 6 feet tall and had white-blond hair. Going by his unmistakable accent he was a South African. He knelt down beside me. 'I saw you from over there.' He pointed in the direction of six adults about 20 metres away, who all started waving. I waved back and nodded my head, smiling.

'They're my family – parents, aunties and uncles. We saw you in the wheelchair by yourself and I wanted to help a fellow Christian,' he confidently remarked. I was about to ask how he figured I was Christian then remembered my crucifix tattoo. I would often forget about the tattoo on my leg, which I had gotten because I thought it looked good and not to initiate discussions about Christianity.

He handed me a cake, the same kind the protestors had given me.

'I don't want this. Would you like it?' I always thought people were a pain in the arse if they tried to talk to me and I didn't know them. I liked to be left alone, something I got from my dad. Growing up, I would often see him avoid people and situations that warranted small talk.

'I just want to be left alone. I hate bullshit small talk, it's all crap,' he would say after I asked him why he avoided things. Hearing that for so many years rubbed off on me, I supposed. It was a hard habit to break.

'I would love to help you in any way I can,' my South African buddy said.

'Thanks, man, I appreciate it,' I said, trying to also convince my inner negative thoughts.

While sitting down listening to him talk about Christianity I began to get anxious for Ruben's return. There's only a limited amount of time you can listen to someone and pretend you care about what they're saying. Don't get me wrong: at the time I appreciated Christianity and believed certain things, but getting preached to in the situation I was in was hard to accept.

'I have an idea,' he said. 'Do you believe in instant healing?'

I had no idea what he was talking about. He noticed.

'Jesus was able to instantly heal through prayer and it has also been done by others.'

'Ah, instant healing, I didn't really hear what you said. Yeah, I believe it.' Lying once again so I didn't look stupid or hurt his feelings.

After visiting the Buddhist temple and being able to feel what was being said, at this stage in my life I didn't know what I believed. Instant healing was not one of them, though.

'Okay, perfect, let's do it,' he said, as he leaned in, placed my injured leg in both of his arms and knelt on the ground. My South African prophet closed his eyes and put his face close to my leg and began muttering prayers. I was so embarrassed looking around at people watching him.

Please, Jesus! I thought, *don't let Ruben come back now.* I could imagine Ruben's reaction to seeing a guy hugging my leg. I didn't want him to return and reveal that I wasn't as polite and religious as this young man believed. Looking around for Ruben while the man continued to pray, I noticed his parents and family watching me as if thinking: *Why is he looking around? Why isn't he praying with our boy?*

Again, caring what others thought, I closed my eyes and leant forward, pretending to pray. With my eyes closed I began picturing other people walking past and laughing. My miserable mind bounced straight to thinking that others were ridiculing me.

Who cares what they think? I thought defiantly as I succumbed to just listening to the South African praying. After about one minute I became completely relaxed. My injured leg felt softer as he took the weight, and even shook a little in pleasure.

'How do you feel?' He leant back with a huge smile on his face, as though expecting me to jump up and start doing cartwheels.

'To be honest, it's not fixed but my pain has lessened!'

'Well, it's a start,' he said.

I did feel a lot better. I felt good because this guy was helping me. He snapped me out of the hell I was in for a few moments and I was thankful for such caring actions.

147

It's funny: these days I would love to chat with a guy like this. Somebody who believes in something so much is an awesome person to speak with. They never care what other people think of them, and they never worry about other people's thoughts.

I wished he could instantly heal that about me. These moments throughout my life, praying late at night and listening to Dad speak about Jesus, and even my South African friend – all these things would eventually add up to me finding my path and opening up to the ultimate truth.

I continued looking at him, thinking how much easier and happier his life was compared with mine. He was still kneeling on the white-tiled floor, and he probably would have kept doing so for months if it helped me. Was it him who helped or his religion?

I feel a lot of truth has been lost over time through our obsession with enhancing the ego. When there are fights over whose religion is better people are killed to determine who is the most spiritual. It's like two doctors killing each other over who has kept the most people alive. It's insane! Attachment is the root cause of most pain:

> Attachment to life: scared of death.
> Attachment to a partner: devastated at the thought of being alone.
> Attachment to money: greed and anxiety at the thought of losing it.
> Attachment to a belief: thinking other people's beliefs are wrong causes separation.

> Attachment to a particular country's flag: even this is another form of attachment that results in the separation of humanity.

The ego loves attachment. Have you ever tried to meditate or pray and all you can feel is your loud mind chirping away? That's the ego knowing you're in the process of separating from it and detaching yourself from your thoughts. The ego is scared of this, knowing that if you slow your thinking and allow your true self, your spirit, to shine then the ego will have its powers over you lessened.

I often listened to my dad telling us to 'trust in Jesus'. He would also go on telling us about the church he attended at Sydney's Town Hall on Sundays for mass and during the week for Bible study. I loved that Dad found religion as it kept him sane and calm, mostly. It helped in those times when he would normally snap. He still loses his temper occasionally, but now at least he reflects on it afterwards.

'So, you continue to pray, Luke, every day and it will get fixed,' my white-blond, kneeling friend said.

'I do pray every day,' I proudly responded. I did pray, often speaking to whomever was listening and asking for things I wanted. This was genuine and I think he could feel it, as he smiled brightly once again. There were a few thousand people walking around and many tourists lying down and using their suitcases as pillows, not knowing what to do. In that moment, though, it felt like I was at home on my couch chatting to an old friend, that's how comfortable he made me feel.

'I will give you one last prayer before I go,' he announced as he bent down to hug my leg again.

'What the fuck is going on here? Who's this cunt?' I heard from over my right shoulder. We both looked up as Ruben grabbed his suitcase.

'Ruben, this is . . . Sorry, man, I don't even know your name.' I hoped the introduction would make him forget about what Ruben had just said.

'It's Xavier,' he said, standing up from his crouched position.

'Ruben, this is Xavier, he's from South Africa.' Ruben shook his hand lightly without looking at him.

Xavier wrote down his email address on my cardboard drug bag. He asked that I email him to let him know that all was well and to keep in touch. I later lost that bag in Bangkok, something I regret to this day. If you are reading this, Xavier, all is well.

Ruben placed our suitcases across my thighs and my crutches on top of those. As he started pushing me I could barely see over the top. 'Hey, I spoke with our insurance company,' Ruben said from behind as he continued to push.

'Yeah, big help they are,' I sarcastically responded.

'Nah, they cover when shit like this happens,' Ruben continued. 'They are going to pay for a hotel close to here. They want a place close 'cause they reckon we will be going home tomorrow.'

'Tomorrow?' I said, shocked. 'Man, I need to go home now!' I felt my spirit leave my body.

'Tomorrow,' he responded softly.

I was pushed to the back of a line of people waiting for taxis, and almost an hour later Ruben helped me into the back of one.

My leg was getting really irritated and uncomfortable. Driving through thick clouds of pollution in the heat and smell felt like a punch in the face. We only travelled for a few minutes before we arrived at our destination.

A crappy hotel room was like a five-star retreat from the commotion of the airport and streets. Ruben pushed open the jammed door to our room.

'What a shit hole,' he said, before turning around to push me in, still with the suitcases across my thighs. As we entered the room I looked across the pale orange walls to the bed linen and curtains, which all matched in the same nauseating colour. I climbed onto the bed and heard noises outside as if we were a helicopter pad and were being landed on every couple of minutes. The noise of the streets in Bangkok is of sounds I'd never heard. It's complete chaos.

Ruben was in the toilet when his phone rang. He sprinted out after flushing the toilet and while still pulling his pants up.

'Hello,' he answered. 'Ah, yes, yes, please. Thank you,' he continued, speaking in a girly, child-like voice. Whenever he tried to sound respectable or nice he would put on a voice that was the total opposite of himself. After a few minutes he began answering questions.

'Yes, it's been like five days. The surgeon said the plates and everything went well. He's got heaps left,' he told the caller as he looked through my drug bag. Ruben was speaking to a doctor from Australia whom the insurance company had asked to call us, and he was asking different questions to try to gauge the condition I was in.

'I'm not doing that,' Ruben said, scrunching up his face. 'Man, are you serious?' he went on.

What does this guy want Ruben to do? I thought. Insane scenarios entered my mind such as Ruben having to use a thermometer in places I didn't want him to go. He was looking at me while he leaned on the doorway between my bed and the bathroom. He walked over to me while still holding the phone to his ear then he reached over, keeping his body at a distance like he didn't want to get too close, and squeezed my big toe. I felt a pinch for a few seconds. He then ran into the bathroom and washed his hands.

'Yeah, it's heaps white,' he answered the man's question before handing the phone to me.

'Okay, Mr Kennedy,' the doctor said. 'I wanted your brother to squeeze the big toe on your injured leg to see if it changed colour, which means there is still blood circulating. If not it could mean a bad infection, which I desperately hope to avoid,' he said sternly.

'What's the worst that could happen if it got infected?' I asked, concerned.

'The worst, Mr Kennedy, is that you could die.'

All Ruben wanted was to avoid touching my toe.

'You must keep it elevated to avoid swelling, and –'

I interrupted him. 'It's already swollen.'

'Okay, well –' he tried to continue.

'It's heaps itchy too,' I butted in. I was now worried.

'Okay, Mr Kennedy, I know you have been moving around. It's imperative you move as little as possible and keep your leg elevated. What's the dressing like?' he asked.

'What do you mean?'

'The bandages on your leg: are they covering the wound properly?'

'Yeah, it's covered fine but blood is seeping through it,' I said. The line was silent. 'Hello?' I asked, thinking the international call had dropped out.

'Yes, I'm here, Mr Kennedy. You must keep your leg elevated and do not travel unless totally necessary. Because there's blood coming through the dressing I want you to go to the nearest hospital tomorrow and get it redressed.'

Now he was worried. First he had told me it was imperative I move as little as possible, then he said I had to go to the hospital. I was petrified.

If a doctor is concerned then something must really be wrong.

Since arriving at this run-down, seedy and depressing hotel I had been fretting that the people from Pattaya would find us. Our names were on the hotel registry and I could imagine them going from hotel to hotel to hunt us down. They would know that we hadn't gotten our flight because of the airport drama. We were stuck in this orange box in a foreign land with a mob of angry people wanting our blood. Flicking through the channels on the television helped very little. I couldn't find much in English, and whatever I could find was shockingly grim. The news reports were graphic, worse than a horror movie. It was real life.

They would report on somebody killed by gun shot and show the scene along with the victim and the new-found holes in his body. It was these same sorts of news reports that had a few days earlier shown me with the bones sticking out of my leg. I'm not sure why, but Thai people don't view death as Westerners do. It's kind of a taboo subject for Westerners: we are scared of it and don't want our children to talk about it or see a dead body. In Thailand it's right there in your face on the prime-time news. I believe it may be due to Westerners not being so confident about what happens when we die, but the Thais are in tune with their spirituality and I guess are relaxed in knowing that when they die it's not the end.

I'm forever wondering about life after death. I look at the Thais and wished that I had that surety about what happens.

Death amazes and scares the fuck out of me at the same time.

So here we were stuck in a seedy hotel in a foreign country and running from people who, we thought, were hunting us down for their money – and me with a busted leg, Ruben at the end of his wits and hundreds of thousands of people starting a coup and shutting down our only way home.

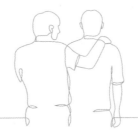

Chapter 10

BROTHER LOVE

Thursday, 27 November; six days after the accident

My spirits were still reasonably high at this stage. Sure, I was terrified of being taken by the angry mob, but it was only one night we needed to avoid them for then we would be in the safety of Australia.

'I'm off, bro,' Ruben said as he put the hotel key in his pocket.

'Where are you going?'

'Out. There are a few bars I went to last time I was here.'

'Man, I wish I could come.'

'Yeah,' Ruben said, pulling a face as if to imply he felt sorry for me. 'See ya,' he said, smiling.

'Later,' I mumbled back.

I upped my dose of painkillers, and after an hour of staring at the ceiling I drifted off to sleep.

When I woke up the next morning Ruben was asleep in the bed next to mine. His phone began to ring.

'Ruben, Ruben! Wake up.'

He woke with a groan and answered his phone. It was an official from Australia.

He slouched over the side of the bed with his head in his left hand and the phone in his right. He was definitely feeling the effects of his big night out.

'Yeah, okay,' he muttered, and hung up the phone. 'They said we aren't leaving today, hopefully tomorrow.' He threw his phone onto the bed and retired his limp body back on the stained white sheets.

'Ah, that's bullshit!' I said back.

'What the hell do you want me to do?' he mumbled.

I was set on going home and was crushed to hear it wasn't happening.

My complaints about not going home were soon erased as I sat up a little to look down at my leg. Yellow and red soup-like fluid was seeping through the bandage and had smeared across the white bed sheets. My leg felt itchy, and behind that itch was a throbbing pain. The oozing pus sickened me.

'Hey, I've got to go hospital to get my dressing redone.'

'Man, are you serious?' Ruben replied out the side of his mouth as his face was smeared across the pillow. He dozed off back to sleep.

I watched him for an hour. I wasn't really thinking about anything, but for some reason I couldn't stop looking at him. I watched as his chest rose, then with an exhaustion of air it fell. Maybe I was numb to emotion or didn't want to face the reality that we weren't going home, but still I just stared. I was totally present. My mind wasn't clouded as I appreciated the calming sensation of Ruben's breathing, and I slowed my breath to match his.

He's my brother, my blood, I thought. *We are one.*

Even though we argued a lot growing up and never really hung out outside of boxing, he still meant the world to me. Watching him peacefully sleep brought a tear to my eye.

I love you.

That moment was healing to my soul; it's exactly what I needed after hearing the bad news. The silence of the moment and my feeling of love towards him rested my weakened mind, giving me the strength to continue. His phone started ringing again, slapping me out of my meditative state. It pulled him up again into a slouched position over the side of his bed.

'It was the travel insurance company. They still don't know when we will be going home.'

With my mind rested from my few moments of pure quietness, I was able to deal with the shattering information of our interminable stay.

'They are putting us in a nicer place in central Bangkok at least.' Ruben sounded a little happier.

'Sweet. On the way there we can stop by the hospital,' I said to him, hoping his spirits would rise a little more. Changing hotels would also keep us on the front foot from the mob. Going into another hospital would be dangerous, as the Frankenstein-led mob certainly knew I was injured and probably also knew I was still in Bangkok.

Outside our hotel in the busy street, even while struggling to breathe in the thick polluted air, we were still happy to be departing the orange box. We didn't have to wait long before a taxi arrived. The taxi driver pulled the handbrake up, but besides popping the boot from his controls where he was seated he didn't budge. There was me in a wheelchair balancing two suitcases and a set of crutches on my lap. Ruben dragged one suitcase at a time over to the boot as I sat watching, then I called out to the driver, 'Mate, how about some help?'

There was a fly sitting on his cheek, seemingly content to only buzz off on its own terms. The driver made no attempt to swat it away and no attempt to help us. Either this was the laziest man I'd ever seen or he just didn't care. Perhaps he was having a tough day.

I watched him for a little and for a moment tried to imagine what his life was like back home. What left a man so broken? I pictured him sitting at the dinner table in his family home, a pile of bills that his wife had just added to lying on the table before him. He was arguing with her about not being able to pay them while his kids watched them fight. I wondered if couples in Thailand fought about money. I know in Australia people certainly do. In a country as lucky as Australia we can take things for granted when we have them and hate each other when we don't.

Ruben pushed me to the back door, helped me get in then folded the wheelchair and placed it in the boot of our new friend's taxi.

'Can you believe this fucking prick?' I could feel Ruben's tension as he gripped my arm to help me in. He was pissed off.

'How you doing, mate?' I asked the driver, feeling strangely sorry for him after imagining what his deal might be. I wanted the situation to be less daunting for all of us. Ruben jumped in the front seat, glaring at the driver like he wanted to kill him. The taxi was full of little golden Buddhas and smelt of freshly burnt incense. There was no response from the driver at my attempted lightening of the situation. Once again he didn't budge.

'Take us to the hospital,' Ruben demanded as the driver pulled out from the front of our hotel. No one spoke a word the whole way. I didn't mind this too much, as back in Australia I would dread hopping in a taxi because of the belief, made clear by my dad, that small talk was rubbish. I would feel awkward as the driver and I attempted a conversation. The lack of talk in the Thai's cab was welcoming for me, but clearly it ate at Ruben. When we arrived at the hospital we again helped ourselves out.

'You dog!' Ruben shouted at the driver, slamming the door before the man could react. With his face scrunched up in anger Ruben pushed me inside, pulsing with attitude.

We had no idea what to do or who to see. After approaching a couple of people to get some advice we gave up trying. We couldn't understand anyone, and they just stared blankly at us. Ruben sat down next to me, exhaling a heavy sigh.

We had been in Thailand for six days. It felt like six years.

My body was aching, and my skin was a blistering white and lips a cracking purple. My health was the worst it had ever been. My diet all week had been almost nothing but drugs and room- service ice-cream, so you can imagine what my insides must have been like. My face was gaunt and my jaw was getting worse; every time it moved I could hear a crunch and click.

Just above my backside were bleeding and painful bedsores because my tail bone was rubbing on either an uncomfortable wheelchair, a hard hospital bed, an irritating hotel bed or the cramped back seat of a taxi. I had bruises everywhere. Worst of all, my leg was still swelling. It had swollen to a sickening dark purple and was also now extremely itchy.

'Can I help you?' a nurse asked in perfect English.

She must have noticed Ruben slouched and me looking close to death and thought, rightfully, that we needed help. I explained what had happened and what I needed, and she escorted me away to another room.

'I'll wait here,' Ruben said.

'Sir, this isn't good. It looks infected. I want you to stay here,' she told me with an uneasy look on her face. She fixed me up with a new dressing and fresh bandages.

'I can't, we are going home soon,' I said, looking out the door at Ruben, who was leaning with his head against a wall in the waiting room.

'There's no way we could stay here, we can't afford it. Besides, I would need to speak with Ruben, he's been a bit down and that will get to him,' I said to the nurse, not taking my eyes off Ruben.

'What will get to him?' she asked.

'I've ruined the trip. I just don't want to disappoint him even more.'

'It's your health, how will you disappoint him?' she queried.

I've ruined his idea of the perfect trip away for us, I thought as I looked out at Ruben. *That first night was great, dancing with him and watching him laugh. Why did I have to push it? Why did I have to keep going? Fucking idiot! No wonder he's pissed off. I had stuffed everything.*

'He just gets a little angry sometimes, that's all. It's been a tough trip. We've had some arguments and everything has been pretty hectic.'

She looked out at him then back at me, and said 'Wait here' before exiting the room, closing the door behind her.

I wheeled my chair over to the door and opened it slightly to see what she was doing.

She was standing next to Ruben and tapping him on the arm, getting his attention.

'Is he ready?' Ruben asked, sitting higher in his seat.

'He is. I just wanted to speak to you,' the nurse continued.

'What's wrong? Is Luke okay?' Ruben asked. I could hear genuine concern in his voice.

I suppose he does care.

Leading up to this I believed Ruben was just annoyed at the predicament I had gotten us into. He never shared his thoughts and emotions, I guess because he thought it made him look weak and vulnerable. Thinking I couldn't hear what he was saying, he allowed me a glimpse into his thoughts.

'No, no, everything is okay with Luke. I just want to see how you are doing,' I heard her say.

'I'm sweet, there's nothing wrong with me,' Ruben said defensively, still unaware I was listening in.

'He said you were angry.'

'What? Has he been in there bitching about me?' Ruben asked, his tone shifting.

'No, not at all. By the sounds of things your brother really looks up to you. He didn't want to make any decisions before speaking to you first,' she said.

I watched as a little smile crept its way across Ruben's face. 'Look, it's just been a hard few days. I love my brother, I would do anything for him. It's just been tough. When I first heard he got in the accident I was absolutely crushed, he's my brother,' Ruben continued as I listened in. It was the first time I had heard Ruben talk about his emotions, and it was also the first time I heard him say he loved me.

'I wanted to bring him to Thailand to show him everything. I feel like we missed out on that,' he went on. 'Look, don't go thinking I'm a bad person because I lose my temper sometimes, I would still do anything for my family,' he reinforced to the nurse.

'Nice to hear,' she said, as she turned and headed back to me. She noticed the door was open on her return. 'I'm glad you heard that,' she said as she entered the room.

Afterwards there was some confusion about payment. I was so used to getting things done back home and just leaving; thank God for Medicare. In Thailand, though, everything came at a cost.

'Bro, we only have a few hundred Aussie left but can cover it. We need to get more cash from home if we are going to be here for few more days,' Ruben said while looking down at me seated in my wheelchair.

'Few more days? No way, we're going home soon, man!'

I said, wishing.

'Hope so.'

'Excuse me, sir, again, you must pay before you are allowed to leave,' the softly spoken nurse behind the counter repeated.

'Yes, one second,' Ruben shot back before looking back at me. 'We need to get more money,' he said, as he pulled notes out of his pocket.

After sorting it all out and having another reduction in our already dwindling budget we were ready to go to our new 'better' hotel the travel insurance had promised. I felt incredible: I was in the worst of situations, but after hearing what Ruben had said about me to the nurse it was one of the happiest moments of my life.

'Here comes another fuckhead taxi driver,' Ruben said as the taxi pulled up. 'I bet he doesn't help either.'

'What's up, boys?' the driver asked, bouncing out of his door and running around to grab the suitcases.

I looked up at Ruben as he glanced down at me at the same time, the two of us grinning together, sharing a secret joke.

'What?' the taxi driver asked, looking back and forth at the two of us.

'Nothing,' Ruben said with a laugh, grabbing the other suitcase to help.

'Where we off to, guys?' the driver asked when we were seated. Ruben gave him the address of the hotel. 'Too easy,' he said, and we started moving. 'You boys don't mind if I play my beats?' he asked, leaning towards his stereo.

I wasn't too keen on listening to Thai music but he was a nice guy so we didn't object. Some old school hip-hop music that both Ruben and I love blared out of the speakers. The three of us sang along like old buddies without a care in the world.

If only.

Ruben sang through fits of laughter, and the difference between the two taxi rides wasn't lost on me. Earlier I could feel Ruben's energy, and felt the taxi would explode from his built-up tension. Even after getting out of the car Ruben pushed my wheelchair with gusto, the driver's unhelpful actions staying with him and making him angry. It reminds me of an old story I heard . . .

Two monks were making a pilgrimage to venerate the relics of a great saint. During the course of their journey they came to a river where they met a beautiful young woman, an apparently worldly creature dressed in expensive finery and with her hair done up in the latest fashion. She was afraid of the river's current and of ruining her lovely clothing, so asked the brothers if they would carry her across the river.

The younger and more exacting of the brothers was offended at the very idea and turned away with an attitude of disgust. The older brother didn't hesitate and quickly picked the woman up on his shoulders, carried her across the river and set her down on the other side. She thanked him and went on her way, and the brother waded back through the waters.

The monks resumed their walk, the older one in perfect equanimity and enjoying the beautiful countryside while the younger one grew more and more brooding and distracted, so much so that he could keep his silence no longer and suddenly burst out, 'Brother, we are taught to avoid contact with women

164

and there you were, not just touching a woman but *carrying her on your shoulders!*'

The older monk looked at the younger one with a loving, pitiful smile and said, 'Brother, I set her down on the other side of the river. You are still carrying her.'

Ruben was the happiest I'd seen him since I had jumped into the hot tub naked, and while I was thrilled to see my dear friend, my brother, having a shift in his disposition it was hard to turn away from the fact that he was letting some stranger determine his mood. A five-minute taxi ride was able to make him angry or happy. Seeing moments like this on our trip had woken up something in me, because I lived my whole life like this. Up and down, relaxed or tense, happy or sad, calm or mad: all driven from outer sources. Watching the world and what happens in it determined how I felt.

These days, whenever I'm reflecting on days in the past I sometimes think back to a single, tiny unimportant thing. We all do this: an off comment made by someone in passing, sometimes a friend, sometimes a stranger and suddenly an entire day is ruined because you're stuck focusing on that one little moment.

When we caught up with friends we could have a lunchtime filled with laughs, but afterwards I would be stuck in my head reliving each comment made or story I told, and I would convince myself that I shouldn't have said what I said or spoken so much and I would wonder if my friends still thought highly of me.

I try my best to capture those reactions and pull myself away from them. Don't let these moments overshadow your joy. Don't live your life in reaction to other people.

Be you.

We arrived at what looked like a beautiful white palace: this hotel was indeed an improvement on the last. The driver helped me out while humming the song we had just been singing. There couldn't have been a better example of contrast than that between this sparkling white building and the public areas of Bangkok, their limbless beggars on the footpaths, three-legged wild dogs barking and fighting each other, polluted air as thick as pea soup, tuk-tuks jostling for positions, hustlers trying to con tourists and clogged-up sewerage everywhere.

I sat in my wheelchair as Ruben pushed me through wide doors that were opened by a man waiting inside. 'Good afternoon, gentlemen,' he said as we passed. We both nodded our heads.

Another man in a sharp, dark red suit and slick, long black hair fetched our luggage from the taxi and placed it on a gold-trimmed trolley before accompanying us inside. As we entered the doors the fresh cool air of the lobby was a welcoming escape from the sticky, humid, smelly outside air. The sounds of car horns and engines were replaced with the sounds of a man playing a piano and being supported by a violinist standing to his right. They were on a mini stage surrounded by guests, and a few of the guests were watching the performers while sipping on cups of tea. One was reading his native country's newspaper. Two men who looked Russian were leaning in towards each other over a table, obviously not wanting people to hear their business. Four Japanese men were all on one side of a table looking through folders and chatting intently.

One older man was with a sexy brunette woman who looked to be half his age. They were sitting on a banana-shaped white leather couch that looked to be 20 metres long. The man had large gold rings on each finger, his grey hair was gelled back and golden sunglasses sat on the top of his head. He took a phone call and began speaking loudly, which seemed to disappoint his female friend. She went to kiss him but he leaned away to avoid it as he continued speaking on the phone. She looked away and swiped his hand off her knee. He attempted to speak on the phone again.

'You always talking,' she said in a European accent before rolling her eyes.

All these people looked important and extremely wealthy.

Surrounding the foyer was a freshly cut garden with striking, bright-coloured flowers. It was one of the richest gardens I had ever seen. A large marble water fountain and running stream parted the plantation to make way for a trickle of water that was beautiful in its gentle flow. The water added to the breathtaking sounds of the piano and violin and made what I was hearing seem spiritual.

The smells of the flowers, the feeling of cool fresh air and the magical sounds allowed me to be submerged in the moment. I felt at peace. It was ultimate pleasure.

My thoughts were gone.

The feeling was a direct opposite to what I had been going through the last few days, and suddenly I felt tears in my eyes. Tears of hope. Tears that told me everything was going to be okay.

It was another boost for my hidden spirit. It seemed these moments of solace were occurring exactly when I needed them.

I felt as though I was being looked after, but by what?

I couldn't see much from the reception counter, being so low to the ground in my wheelchair. I could only make out the foreheads of a man and lady, both of whom spoke fluent English and were giving Ruben information about our room.

'Names, sir?' the man asked.

I grabbed Ruben and pulled him down close to me. 'Give them a fakey.' I didn't want the mob to find us here.

'You idiot, they already have our names down.' He shrugged free of my grip to stand straight up and continue speaking. He was given the keys to our room and we were led by two of the men in the red suits, one with our luggage and the other pushing me. As we passed through the lobby I could see the older man with the slick grey hair was still speaking loudly on his phone, but he was alone.

Just . . . be . . . silent . . .

At this point in my life, as a 23 year old, I didn't know where I was heading. My dream was the navy and I hoped it was something that would right some of my wrongs, that it could be my way of giving back.

I wasn't going to be giving back anything, though, by enlisting, and I knew it. It was just me being selfish again. I wanted to be looked at as a better person. Was I a better person for enlisting or did I just want to fool people into believing so?

When I had made up my mind to join I listened to Mum in the kitchen telling family members that her boy was joining the navy. I could tell how proud she was and this made me feel good. I wasn't doing it to fight for my country, I was doing it to feel better about myself. Another thing to, yet again, enhance my ego. At least this enhancement had positive outcomes. So as a young man and with what I had already been through I was certain I had it in me to be something big. Even though I was lazy with a lot of things, if I put my mind to something I wanted I got it.

I would always go for greatness at whatever expense. I had to win at absolutely any cost.

As we entered our room I looked straight at the bed. *Here we go again*, I thought, as I hopped on one leg and slowly lowered myself down. The whole bed thing was getting to me, not only because of my leg but also because of the friction sores on my tail bone. I was so used to training every day and being out and about, and normally the only time I would be in bed all day was when recovering from a big bender. The only sores I would have were inside my mouth from chewing gum, my reaction to all the speed or pills.

Ruben didn't stick around for long. 'I'm off,' he said.

I watched him exit the room and smiled, knowing he really did care but he just didn't know how to show it.

I found that after our hour-long trip I had to put my leg up straight away. Short as the journey had been, it took a toll. Placing my leg on top of our bag was the only way I could keep it properly elevated. I glanced down at my leg: it was getting worse.

I tried to get situated and comfortable, but even on the short trips to the toilet my leg would swell up and become intensely painful. I could only see half the television because no matter what angle I tried to position myself in my leg left me on my side. I searched through the channels anyway and found one playing something in English. I resigned myself to the fact that I would spend this day with my new three amigos: bed, drugs and room-service ice cream.

The drugs were working, but I found myself having to use twice as many as I drifted in and out of sleep in a foggy haze of pain.

I was running out. Like a junky, it powerfully worried me. I was using the drugs to dull everything: my stabbing pain, loud thoughts and waking hours. I needed them. Without them I would have to face reality. I knew I had an addictive personality, but prescription pills were something I never thought would get a hold of me. Were they?

'Knock, knock.'

There was a knock at the door, and I froze and was taken out of my drug-fuelled stupor. *The mob!* I thought as there was another, harder knock on the door. Ruben had his keys, so it wasn't him.

I thought that it was about time they found us, and I remember doing quick calculations of how much money we had and hoping they would accept my apologies and take it. We were down to a couple of hundred Australian dollars so had nowhere near the amount I owed.

'Lume servacce!' I heard a loud voice say as harder knocks hit the door. 'Lume servacce!' the man hollered more loudly.

'What the fuck is lume servacce?' I muttered to myself. Then it dawned on me that this was their gang name and I was finished!

This situation was one I couldn't control. I couldn't afford to pay them, and I really hoped the bike lady was insured and wished that the injured lady wasn't injured. I hopped up and grabbed my crutches. *Could I use them as a weapon?*

'Knock, knock!'

The beating on the door was now deafening as I gripped the doorknob and slowly turned it. I tried to put on a brave face, waiting to be kidnapped or killed on the spot.

'Lume servacce,' a man said as he gently held a silver tray.

I smiled.

This little man in his broken English saying 'Room service' had me as scared as a little kid opening a cupboard expecting Freddy Krueger.

If it had been the mob I would have been cut up a lot more than what Freddy could have managed. I had ordered ice-cream before I fell asleep and forgotten about it.

The man carried the plate into my room and stood there as I fell slowly back onto the bed. I usually forgot about tipping, but this time I practically threw money at him. I was incredibly happy and showed it, and he walked away probably thinking *'That man must love his ice cream.'*

The day went by full of bad dreams, bad television, bad gas and bad mistakes. I wanted a sleep that wouldn't drift from real life to bad dreams. This was tripping me out. I couldn't tell the difference between the two; they just blended into each other. I decided to more than double my dose of painkillers and hope for a deep sleep. I was petrified of the dreams I was having. I was also scared of the reality I was in.

As I popped the pills I pictured myself being found dead on the bed. I shrugged this thought off as I gulped water and waited for the pills that were now in my stomach to take effect.

Chapter 11

TWO EGOS CLASH

Friday, 28 November

'Man! Man! Come on, come on!'

I woke up and couldn't feel my right arm. Ruben was shaking me and screaming. He stank of alcohol.

'Luke!' he cried.

'What?' I asked back, shaking off the sleep.

'What the fuck did you do, bro? I've been trying to wake you for ten minutes. I got back last night but didn't want to wake you. You were in the exact same position this morning when I woke up.'

It was the next day, and even though Ruben had had some sleep he was still drunk. I had taken the pills the previous afternoon and hadn't moved a centimetre since. I still couldn't feel my right arm. I lifted it with my left and started shaking it. It looked dead. I had fallen asleep on it, for who knows how long. A few scared minutes later I had a little feeling and movement.

'Man, I didn't see all the empty tablet packets last night. I noticed them this morning and freaked out, and when you wouldn't wake up I thought you fucking OD'd!' Ruben said, trying to hide his tears.

After realising I was okay he was soon back to sleep. I tried to get comfortable, hoping for some good news about us heading home. I still felt intoxicated by the pills and was dead still, only moving to grab the remote control, which had found its way in between Ruben's bed and mine. I switched to the only channel that was playing English.

Credits were running from a movie that had just finished.

Hoping for something entertaining to lift my spirits, I was disappointed when I saw a large man get hit by a car that was being chased by police. It was the same movie from the day before and was being played at the same time. The next movie was also the same as the day before, as was the one after that.

My only form of entertainment, the only thing that was keeping my mind from chattering away and going insane, was playing the same thing.

Please get me home.

The phone rang and I answered it. 'Hello?'

It was the official we had been in touch with from Australia. 'You guys are coming home tomorrow.'

My prayers had been answered!

'Bangkok still has no access but an airport not far from there will be accessible,' the man told me.

A massive relief washed over me, and I felt as though a weight had been lifted off my body. I remember feeling very light and couldn't wait for Ruben to wake up.

'Bro, we are going home tomorrow,' I yelled the moment his eyes flickered a little.

'I wanted to go home today,' he said, as he woke up into his recurring hangover slouch over the side of the bed.

'Nah, I just spoke to the guy from back home.' I went on to explain how we were flying out of a different airport.

Shortly after Dad called, and you could hear the excitement in his voice. Mum jumped on the phone, and she was extremely happy as well. The whole time we had been there Dad had wanted to get on a flight over. If it hadn't been for us being told we were flying home the next day he would have been straight over somehow. It would have been nice to have him there.

'Man, we have no money.' Ruben dropped a bombshell.

'What do you mean we have no money?' I asked, confused.

'We've run out. Your bandages and drugs cost us heaps.'

Right. This coming from the guy who had gone out partying day through night. I knew where most of the cash had gone.

'You have been going out, bro!' I said slowly, still not sure I wanted to go through with what I said.

'Well, what do you want me to do? Sit here all day while you're on drugs? Are you saying you would stay here all day if it were you?' he asked defensively.

'Whatever,' I returned, knowing there was some truth to what he was saying. 'Anyways, what are we going to do?' I asked sceptically as the non-existence of our cash pissed me off, although his justification lessened that.

'Man, I thought we were going home today so I spent the last of it,' Ruben responded. Would I have done the same if

I had thought we were heading home? Probably. Admittedly we didn't need much money, as travel insurance was covering our buffet breakfast and we were going home the next day.

'I'm hungry,' Ruben said, as he jumped up.

Remembering we had a buffet breakfast, Ruben couldn't wait to get downstairs and hose off some of his hangover.

'I'm coming!' I said, enthusiastically. 'Man, I'm starving. I haven't been hungry for anything other than ice cream for days. I am now, though.'

I felt like a kid on an excursion. I had only been in that room for one night but in that time I had experienced the worst dreams imaginable, a terrifying visit from the lume servacce gang member, the same three movies on repeat, a near overdose on painkillers, more unbearable pain from my leg, the constant ache of the sores on my tail bone and, oh, the *great* news that we were heading home the next day.

I couldn't believe it had only been one night, as the drugs made my sense of time unreliable.

We entered the buffet. 'Hey, brother, push me around so I can grab my food,' I asked Ruben.

'Fucking hell,' he moaned.

'Are you serious?' I asked as he gripped the back of my wheelchair.

As he pushed me over to the food my anger towards him was replaced with eagerness as I was now gliding across light blue tiles that separated the buffet section from the hotel's pearly white tiles. As I was being pushed along I could see the buffet counters were enormous.

Everything was glowingly clean and the food looked super fresh. Red lobsters, succulent orange prawns, whole cooked fish and sushi set out in immaculate rows of four looked too perfect to touch let alone eat. This seafood table was the best I had ever seen.

The next table had Thai food. Another, Italian. The dessert table had green and red jelly with a side bowl of fresh cream. The detail that went into everything was amazing; it all looked fake. Fresh fruit was scattered around everywhere for eating but also for decoration.

'Come on,' I heard from behind. I couldn't pick much because of Ruben's moans and groans for me to hurry up. Ruben left me back at our table to fetch his own food. Each mouthful of food I tasted was like I was biting down on a piece of enchanting happiness. I would normally eat very fast, but after not eating proper food for days I was savouring every moment. Even though my jaw was hurting, my full attention was on the abundance of flavours waltzing in my mouth. I could taste each bite of food. I had a slice of pizza and I could taste the dough, different meats, onion, mushrooms and vegetables all individually even though I had a mouthful of everything at once. It was bizarre. I was present. My mind would normally be berserk as I ate and I would often look down to realise I had finished without even really tasting my food. This time was different. I appreciated every bite.

After only eating ice cream and swallowing drugs for a few days I was grateful for the food I would usually just eat and run from without giving it a second thought. Gratitude is one of the highest emotions, because when you're grateful every negative or anxious thought process is put away and what remains is genuine happiness. When you're grateful you're focusing on a single positive thought. For the first time in my life I was genuinely thankful for what I was eating.

It's like in meditation when you bring your attention to your breath to gain presence. My thoughts focused on each mouthful. I envisioned every bit of food touching my tongue as my teeth chewed. The bits of food, although mixed up, were each in their own taste-filled cocoon. Their exploding flavours were each revealed as they bounced onto my taste buds.

Our loud thoughts hide so much of what's going on in this world. I wonder what else we fail to notice.

Just . . . be . . . silent . . .

Ruben returned and started to eat his food. 'How nice is this!' I exclaimed, trying to spark up a conversation. Ruben nodded and kept eating. After finishing his plate he got up to get more food.

'Can you push me around?' Like him, I wanted another plate of this amazing food.

'Nah, fuck that. What do you want to get? I'll grab it,' Ruben said in his dismissive tone. We were at the end of the road with each other. Despite the warmth I'd seen earlier in the hospital, he was angry.

'Come on, man, I'll be quick,' I attempted.

'Alright,' Ruben replied, his mood softening a little. 'But fuck this trip! I'm over this shit,' he continued. 'And what the fuck are you looking at?'

I thought Ruben was talking to me, but then I heard the scratch of a chair behind me.

'I'm looking at you. Do you have a problem?' an unfamiliar voice said. I turned in my wheelchair to see a tall European sporting a Mario-like moustache and wearing suit pants and a collared business shirt. His jacket hung over the back of his seat. His clothes were attempting to hide tattoos I could see peeking out of a gap in the buttons of his shirt. This same shirt had wet patches in the armpits.

As I stared at this man and thought, *Who the fuck does this guy think he is?* I felt my body tense up. It was conditioned to prepare for battle when involved in a confrontation such as this. I wanted to jump up and attack him. *Why is all this shit happening? Who is this guy? What happened?*

Ruben hadn't reacted yet so I relaxed my tension a little, thinking this would go nowhere. Then I heard the screeching of chair legs on the tile floor. Ruben was taking the man's bait.

Both men stood as though they had invisible basketballs under their arms in an attempt to look bigger than they were. I was stuck in between them as they continued to stare at each other.

'Do you want to have a go?' Ruben broke the silence.

'Don't let this suit fool you, I will mess you up,' the man said.

'Well, let's go, you fucking dog.'

'Hey, pull up both of you!' I snapped from my seated position. When seeing a family member or friend in trouble my initial reaction was attack, as my body and mind could be taken over by rage and any sensible thought patterns would be wrestled into submission by a vulgar ego. But this time after releasing my tension through thinking nothing was going to happen, I realised the best thing to do was to try reason these two out of a fight.

* * *

I wonder how many people are now lying in a gaol cell, hospital bed or coffin after being taken over by immediate rage. If they had given in to just a few seconds of stillness their lives would've taken a completely different road, or those who had been killed in a fleeting rage could be living peacefully. I once saw a friend of mine, Kane, in a horrific incident when he was taken over by rage. Kane was a true gentleman, the first to get up to offer his chair to a female or take his jacket off when someone was cold. This one night was different. We had been seated in a pub and Kane got into an argument with another man, who punched Kane before the scuffle was broken up by security. As he was being held back by security I could see the rage in Kane's eyes. His breaths were short as he growled through his teeth.

'We will get him when he leaves,' I whispered as we were all escorted out. Kane was fuming. The guy who had punched Kane could be heard inside laughing.

'Fuck him,' Kane roared.

'Relax, brother, we will get him when security aren't around,' I tried to reason.

'You think you're tough trying to fight my boyfriend?' I heard a drunken woman's voice say.

I looked over and saw a lady stumbling towards Kane.

'Go away, your man is inside. Just fuck off,' I said to her, hoping she would leave Kane be.

'Yeah, piss off!' Kane barked before turning around to walk away.

The girl punched Kane in the back of the head. Ignition.

In a split second Kane turned and in one movement brought his elbow up and slammed it into the girl's jaw. It switched her lights off instantly and her limp body flopped towards the pavement.

'No!' I heard Kane scream in instant regret as he caught the girl. Kane was already crying.

The girl suffered a broken jaw and Kane received a two-year gaol sentence.

That split second of being taken over: what was it? How many times have we said something or done something we didn't mean to say or do in that moment of rage? What is it? Why are some people affected more than others?

It's the loud mind demolishing our pure soul. Rage comes from uncontrollable violent thoughts from the past or present that bounce through our minds, arming every cell of our body. These cells convulse while waiting to explode. The rupture of fury is like a discharge of built-up tension, and discharging the tension creates a sense of release and some pleasure. For a moment there's space, room to breathe as your body tingles in pleasure. No more stress. Your pure being is exposed as reasoning returns, but more often than not it's too late.

Silence the thoughts and create more gaps in thinking and the roaring agitation will lessen.

Just ... be ... silent ...

* * *

'Shut up, cripple,' the suited man said.

'Call my brother a cripple?' With that, Ruben pounced over my left shoulder and punched the man in his cartoon character–like mustached mouth, the force rocking him back onto his table. Plates and cups smashed onto the floor and the man's breakfast ended up being spread across his back.

'I want him arrested. He just punched me!' the man shouted out of his bloody mouth.

'Are you fucking kidding? You act like a tough man then you want to snitch like a bitch?' I laughed. 'Let's go,' I said to Ruben, who stood flexing every muscle as he expected the man to come back to fight. I grabbed him, which snapped him out of his attacking stance, and we headed back to our room while the man still yelled for help.

Even though Ruben was tiring of me, it was good to see he would still back me up.

How did breakfast at a buffet turn to this? Two egos caught each other's eyes and the result was conflict, as it always is with ego. Ruben's eyes were scanning the buffet, as was the other gentleman's. With their minds on food all was okay, but when their eyes met it was as though they had locked on to each other. The energy from both people determined the response, the response determined the reaction and the reaction determined the outcome. External forces again at work.

If Ruben had been scanning the buffet and his eyes had caught those of a woman his mind would have hoped that the girl was interested. An energy of aliveness would have taken him over as his breakfast turned into an opportunity to get laid.

Eyes meeting another set of eyes. Nothing was different in either situation, though the mind's interpretation of what was occurring was the difference between a punch in the face and an erection. Ruben was on edge and irritated about having to be with me in my current state. I know that whenever I gave out that energy it wasn't long before I would find things on the same frequency.

Have you ever had one of those days where everything is going wrong? It may have started with something like getting caught in traffic. Your body would have tensed up and you would have felt annoyed. When you give out that energy your subconscious mind searches for the same thing, and thus a day full of terrible things occurs. Whatever frequency you're on you'll attract more on that same wavelength, which is why living in a state of gratitude not only lifts your mood and reduces your thoughts, but it also attracts more things in your life to be grateful for. The same goes for the other way.

Back in our room and with Ruben far too wired, I had to care for myself. I was incredibly weak, and my arms felt like the red jelly in the buffet. I could barely pull myself out of the chair to hop back into bed. I sat again watching one of the three movies playing on repeat.

Anne called. I spoke to her for about 20 minutes, the conversation limited because Ruben was in the room. After hanging up the phone it rang again straight away.

'We have been trying to call you. Tomorrow is no go, we are still working on getting you home but it's not going to be tomorrow.' It was the consulate official with more bad news. It had been one week since my accident, and I was close to tears. Before that call I'd felt we were so close I could actually see the ocean under our plane. I was sure we were going home and couldn't believe we weren't. Ruben could tell by the look on my face that the news wasn't good.

'Fuck, we have no money!' Ruben exclaimed.

Although insurance covered food we still needed cash for transportation and other living expenses. I was also due for another dressing change on my leg; the bloody pus was seeping through.

'Call Dad.'

After speaking to Dad we ended up getting in contact with our trainer Stan, who wired us $1,000.

Saviour!

'Man, I wonder when we are going home. This is bullshit,' I said, angrily.

'Don't know,' Ruben said as he stood up to look for his wallet. 'I'm going out,' he said when he found it.

'Bro, don't spend all the cash! It has to last,' I said from the bed.

'I'm not. I'm just going out for a couple of drinks. Just a couple,' he said as the door closed behind him.

I was glad he was gone, because the tension in the room was so thick I could almost see it. I heard screeching tires as I glanced at the television to see a large man being run down by a car being chased by police. Again.

I woke up a couple hours later to laughter.

'Oh, fuck,' I heard from Ruben, then the sound of somebody crashing into a wall. I lifted myself up a little and spotted Ruben with not one, but two ladies in his company.

He was drunk again and fell on the bed as he took off his pants. The three of them ended up on the bed playing around. Ruben stopped.

'Hey, hey, hey. Go over and see my brother,' Ruben said to one of them. She looked over at me and I could see her contemplating whether or not to come over to me, a man with his injured leg up on a suitcase and blood oozing through the bandage. She came over tentatively and sat on the side of my bed. I wasn't able to move my leg and was stoned on painkillers. I was in no mood for this.

She awkwardly asked about my leg. I just wanted to be left alone but replied anyway. 'Yeah, I had a bike accident.' I hoped she would just go away.

'Ah, what are you doing? Fucking love stories over there!' Ruben teased from his bed as he threw some rubbish at us. What did he expect me to do: put on a show?

It wasn't long before Ruben passed out. The two ladies started whispering to each other. It wouldn't have made a difference if they had a microphone because I couldn't understand a word they were saying.

'Where our money?' the lady who had been with Ruben said forcefully, getting up off the bed and walking over to me.

The mob got these ladies to find us. Ruben, you fucking idiot bringing them back. Now we are fucked! My mind immediately jumped to the worst.

'He have sex, now he pay money.' They were hookers.

'I don't have any,' I told them.

'We have to get money,' she said.

The way they said this made it sound like a matter of life and death. A picture of a Thai gangster pimp waiting downstairs for his girls entered my mind.

'Ruben!' I screamed. He didn't budge.

It was a mission and painful for me to even get up to go to the toilet, so having to make my way over to his bed to wake him really angered me. I had to stand on my one good leg to shake him awake. My hip was killing me because of the motion, so I gave up and started feeling for the pockets of his blue jeans. I found a bunch of money and gave it to the ladies.

'Is this enough?' It must have been more than enough as they were happy, although not as happy as I was that they were leaving. I hobbled back to my bed to rest. My leg had started throbbing.

I flicked the TV off, unable to focus. I was too angry. I watched my brother's chest rise up and down to the rhythm of his sleep. It was him I was angry at. Ruben had accessed the money from Stan and this was how he had chosen to spend it.

Chapter 12

POSSIBLE AMPUTATION

Saturday, 29 November

Ruben continued sleeping. My anger dissipated, and I stared at the ceiling. After a three-hour staring competition I finally drifted back to sleep. I woke the next morning and looked up at the television, which was showing the same bullshit as the day before and the one before that. We kept the curtains closed, denying the room all natural light. The glow from the television was the only light apart from the bathroom light, which we occasionally switched on. Being in the dark made me feel safer, although it was starting to play tricks with my eyesight.

Even though the same thing was playing over and over on the TV channel I kept it on. The English language was comforting and increased my sense of safety. I felt closer to home. I didn't want to turn it off and be left in the dark with my crazy thoughts and even wilder drug-fuelled nightmares. After the drama at the buffet yesterday I was happy to pay for my food to be delivered to the room. A knock came at the door.

'Who's that?' Ruben asked, startled awake.

'Just room service,' I said. I got up to answer the door; moving wasn't such a difficult thing when it was for my benefit. I rested back in bed with the tray laid on my lap.

'Room service is expensive, bro. Insurance only gave us a bit of money for food,' Ruben moaned from his bed while staring at the ceiling.

'You fuckin' kidding me?' I said.

'What?' he said, sitting up to stare at me.

'You're worried about money for room service and you bring two fucking hookers back?'

'They weren't hookers! I picked them up the bar, you dick!'
'Bullshit! When you passed out they said I had to pay.'

'You didn't give them any, did you? They weren't hookers!' He stood up to grab his wallet.

'Of course I did, they said they had to be paid. I had to go through your pockets.'

'You're fucked. They weren't hookers. They got you good!'

'They got *us*. It's our money.'

'Well, they got *us*. Shouldn't have given them anything.'

I just shook my head and stared at the ceiling.

Ruben got dressed and left me alone again.

I waited through another long day for news about our return home, but none came. The TV watching, eating and boredom were becoming familiar companions. My leg was ghastly; stiff bits of dried-up bloodied bandage hung loose. It worried me a lot.

It was afternoon when I heard the door click and Ruben walked through, returned from his day out. 'Look at this,' I said, pointing to the blood covering the sheets.

Without hesitation Ruben said, 'Let's get you to the hospital.' He was concerned but seemed annoyed. I let it slide, as it was no longer getting to me. I had enough to worry about.

Frustration was simply too draining, I understood that well enough. I would get frustrated too and it would sap my energy as well as the energy of the people around me. It was just selfish.

'I think we should go to a different hospital this time,' I said.

'What for?' Ruben shot back.

'What if the bike and injured ladies find out we visited the last hospital? They might be waiting for us to come back,' I explained.

'You're just fuckin' paranoid,' Ruben enforced.

'Think about it: if you were owed seven grand and knew the pricks were still around you would give it every chance to get it back.'

Ruben was silent.

'Yeah?' I continued.

'Alright, we'll go somewhere else.'

In the lobby Ruben struggled with the receptionist. It wasn't easy to explain in English to a person for whom

English was a second language that we wanted to go to a different hospital. I waited for Ruben, enjoying a moment of peace among the beautiful garden and water fountain. I fell into a deep meditation, the sound of the slowly trickling water filling my mind.

'That was hopeless.' Ruben had ended the conversation, succumbing to the fact that it was useless. No matter how hard he tried to explain the receptionist insisted we go to the same hospital we'd already been to.

'Man, we can't go there,' I begged Ruben.

'Yeah, alright! I saw a doctor's the other day a few streets away,' he reasoned.

He helped me outside, where we waited for a taxi instead of trekking it to the nearby doctor. It was easier than navigating the broken footpaths, sewage puddles and stray animals, not to mention combating the hot, steamy weather.

When we arrived at the doctor's office Ruben pushed my wheelchair through glass doors that separated once we got closer. The entrance to the office had a large fish tank on which little Thai kids were tapping the glass sides.

'Wait here,' Ruben said before approaching the counter.

I sat watching the kids peacefully giggle and play around the tank.

'They reckon it won't be long,' Ruben said when he returned. 'Fuck, they're shit pets to have,' he added, as he looked over at the tank.

'What, kids?' I jokingly responded.

'No, the fish,' Ruben laughed.

'Why do you reckon they're shit to have?'

'They don't react to anything. They don't bark. You can't play with them. They're boring. Fish don't make any noises.'

'Why do you have to have a noise or response from something to enjoy it?'

'Luke Kennedy.' I heard my name being called.

After the doctor had taken my bandage off his eyes bulged a little. He had a concerned look on his face. Different-coloured pus was climbing out of the dark purple gash, which was encased in a white meaty flesh. A stench drifted up to me within seconds of it being revealed. The gruesome wound ran the length of my leg, which looked more like a chewed-up dog bone. Dried blood and little bits of flesh were hanging off sores and scratches. The doctor did the best he could to clean it up.

'You must go hospital, not good, infected probably,' he said.

'I can't, we are going home tomorrow.'

At least, I hoped we were.

'You have to, you may lose leg,' he said, more sternly.

'I'll be home tomorrow. I can't go hospital here,' I said, a little sterner myself. The doctor shook his head as Ruben grabbed the handles of my wheelchair.

Back in bed at the hotel, I watched the large man being hit by the car for what felt the 50th time when the phone rang.

'Luke? Luke?' It was Dad. His strong deep voice brought me a feeling of instant safety. Even though he was across an ocean, when I heard his voice I was at ease.

'How you doing, mate? How is your leg looking?' he asked.

191

'Yeah, it's sweet, Dad.' I looked down and imagined how my amputated leg was going to look. 'We went and got it redressed a few hours ago and doctor said it was fine,' I lied.

'That's good. It's 'cause you're fit, you're a strong healer. You're going to be okay. We are all praying for you back here. The people at Bible study. Luke –' his voice softened and he slowed his pace – 'Luke, you know, mate, trust in Jesus. There are so many people back here praying for you, so many good people. Trust everything is going to be okay.'

That felt right. It felt good.

I handed the phone to Ruben. 'Yeah, all okay. Nah, it's all good,' Ruben said as he rolled his eyes. 'He's okay!' Dad was asking him about me.

I knew Ruben wouldn't want to upset Mum and Dad. Telling them that a doctor recommended I go back to hospital to avoid amputation wouldn't have helped the situation. Mum was already a worried mess. We had been told on several occasions that we would be going home, only to be disappointed. The rollercoaster ride for those back home would have been manic, as the things they were seeing and hearing on the news were filled with mayhem. In reality, all my life was filled with was an arsehole on television repeatedly getting run over and the odd pretend hooker.

Ruben kept talking to Dad. I had to go pee, so I leaned over to grab my crutches from their resting place against the bedside table between Ruben's bed and mine. I slowly made my way to the toilet, every crutch landing sending a shocking pain through my leg and hip. My strength was that of an old hollowed-out tree branch. I felt I was crumbling with every step. I hopped into the bathroom, dropped the crutches and supported myself on the sink so I could look at myself in the mirror.

My face was gaunt from the lack of food and constant drug intake, and my body had slowly begun to eat away at my muscles to get energy. I was a skinny, smelly, weak wreck. My facial hair was longer than it had ever been. My eyes were bloodshot and there were massive, dark purple bags under each of them. My right eye was bruised from the accident but the other I couldn't blame on anything other than lack of sleep, drugs and a huge desire to be home, or were those big purple bags the result of me crying on the inside? Crying tears of pain that I held in and didn't want exposed. It felt like it. I would always try to hold my misery in, but this misery was forcing itself out through my body. My skin colour mirrored dirty ash. At least the tree branch would have a bit of colour.

I leaned down painfully and scrambled to pick my crutches back up. I only just managed it before I possibly had a wet mess to clean. I peed while standing with all of my weight on the crutches, and I noticed I was passing blood in my urine.

What next? I thought. My worries compounded all the more.

I headed back to bed. Ruben was no longer on the phone.

'You didn't tell him about the infection, did you?' I asked him.

'Nah. He asked if you were seriously okay and I told you were sweet. Mum is all fucked up worrying.'

I put my head on my pillow, and for the first time I almost cried as I imagined my beautiful mum crying the tears of pain I had just resisted.

Ruben sensed something was up and turned to check on me. 'Hey, man, you okay'?

I knew my brother cared for me after hearing him speak to the nurse; I knew he loved me. I also knew it was hard for him to show it. 'You okay, brother?' he asked again as he stood up to head over to me.

The phone rang and Ruben turned to grab it but then stopped. 'Hey,' he said.

I turned my face slowly to look directly into his eyes. 'I'm okay, bro, just grab the phone.'

He looked intently into my eyes for a few more seconds. 'We are going to be okay.' He turned to pick up the phone.

'Let me speak,' I said, so Ruben handed me the phone.

'I understand you boys have been in difficult circumstances over there?' It was another government official from back home.

I rolled my eyes, thinking, *What a fucking genius.* The last guy had promised us the world and ended up just handing us an atlas.

'We are getting you home, either tomorrow or Monday.' At least this guy was smart enough to hedge his bets.

I actually believed this one, though, as he sounded definite and like he wouldn't give false hope. He sounded a little like a military general: hard and straight to the point and, hopefully like a general, he would get shit done.

'We might be going home tomorrow!' I said to Ruben.

'Or Tuesday or Wednesday or Thursday or Friday or Saturday or Sunday?' Ruben made his frustration clear. I shrugged my shoulders, confident we would be home soon.

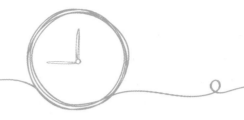

Chapter 13

FOURTEEN HOURS OF TORTURE

Sunday, 30 November

I woke up early the next morning and didn't feel like eating because my jaw was killing me. The clicking had worsened. Even if my jaw was okay I didn't have the energy to eat.

'I think my jaw is broken,' I revealed to Ruben.

He stared at me blankly. 'How's your leg?' he asked after seeing me grimace.

'It's not good. Man, if we aren't going home today . . .' I gave in.

We both stared down at my leg, which was getting worse. I couldn't stand for too long. It was as if all the fluid from my body was draining into my leg, and the pain and uncomfortable

SEX, DRUGS AND A BUDDHIST MONK

stretching of skin made me feel sick. I even had to sit to urinate. If we weren't going home in a few hours I didn't know how I would cope.

I was still staring at my leg when I finally looked up at Ruben. We caught each other's eyes and he awkwardly looked away, lost for words.

'Man, if we aren't going home today I'm just going to go to the hospital and stay there,' I said.

'You can't! They will one hundred per cent find you there!'

'Well, if I don't go I'm going to lose my fucking leg!'

'Better that than your life!' Ruben screamed back.

He was right: I couldn't go to the hospital. If I was found by the mob, even if they didn't hurt or kill me then I would surely be locked up in the infamous Bangkok Hilton for trying to escape without paying.

The Bangkok Hilton is Thailand's Bang Kwang Central Prison, 11 kilometres north of Bangkok. A couple of years before going to Thailand I met a man who had been locked up in this exact gaol for trying to smuggle drugs. He got a 12-year sentence in one of the hardest prisons in the world.

In his book *The Damage Done: Twelve years of hell in a Bangkok prison* Warren Fellows described being thrown in solitary with no light and nothing to eat but rice, so the only way to survive was to reach down beneath the floorboards to grab a whole bunch of cockroaches and eat them. Other stories in the book outlined worse conditions that involved violence, drugs and a lack of hope for a future outside the horrific gaol. This was a place I didn't want to go. I didn't want to end up being killed either, so a hospital stay was a no go.

I was in deep thought about my not-so-sure future when the phone rang. I don't know if it was because I was hoping for the call, but the noise was extra loud – piercing my brain. I was waiting for the call but I didn't want to answer it, and Ruben looked the same. We both glared at the ringing phone as if it was a foreign object. He gave in first and reached for it, pausing before he grabbed it. He looked up at me, shrugged, then finally picked it up.

I held my breath, listening, hoping for the news we were going home. 'Tomorrow, one hundred per cent?' Ruben said after listening for a few seconds.

The word 'tomorrow' felt like he had said 'next year'; tomorrow felt light years away after dealing with all our problems. I was already arguing with Ruben in my head, telling him I couldn't wait until tomorrow. In reality, he kept talking for another 10 minutes. I'd lost the argument to him in my mind so wanted him to get off the phone to hear where we stood. As he hung up I was already pleading my case before he'd put the phone down.

'Man! My leg is fucked, I'm not good. I'm pissing blood, I'm going crazy!'

My desperate pleas couldn't have met a stauncher judge, because there was nothing that could be done. I couldn't do a thing – I was helpless, and we were at the mercy of chance.

'We are nearly there,' Ruben said, trying to sound supportive. He made his point clear without causing an argument and demolishing the last of my energy. I dropped my head into my hands and closed my eyes. I accepted defeat. I shook my head slowly and didn't talk. It was only an extra day away, but I wasn't sure I would make it another night in the state I was in. My mind was giving in, my leg was throbbing, my energy was gone and I couldn't eat.

I just wanted to go home.

'Hey, umm,' Ruben hesitated. There was more to the conversation he'd had, and from his tone I could tell I wasn't going to like it. I could feel my face going red hot; it was boiling but, hey, at least I was probably getting some colour back. I took stock and braced myself for the news.

'We *are* leaving tomorrow but . . .' I looked up at Ruben, my expression hardening. He held his hand up, cautioning me to hold my tongue. '. . . we have to fly out of Phuket.' Taking a breath, he finished what he had to say in a rush. 'We have to get a bus there.'

My stomach dropped. 'I can't get on a bus! My leg doesn't bend, the pain's excruciating if I move it a mil. How the fuck am I going to get on a bus?'

'You can sit in the aisle seat and put your leg up,' he said, matter of factly.

'Really? Like when I put my leg up in the taxi?'

Ruben nodded and smiled.

'Just the motion fucks it up. If it's longer than the taxi ride we had the other day I'm fucked!'

Ruben didn't respond.

'Well, how far away is it?' I said, my voice cracking. The taxi ride had been 20 minutes and the pain had been torturous.

Gently, Ruben spoke. 'Nearly fourteen hours.'

My universe exploded in disbelief. 'No . . .' I said through a sigh. It felt like my soul had been ripped out of me and thrown from our 12th-storey window. My good friend denial kicked in and strengthened by belief that if I willed it hard enough the trip wouldn't happen.

'No way, it's not happening. I'm not going. I'll fucking die on that bus.' I had to convince Ruben.

'Please, Luke, we have to. I'll get you some stronger drugs. We have to, otherwise we can't go home,' Ruben begged.

The only words that registered were 'go home'. The stuff before it was nonsense to me.

'I'll get you some really good drugs, you won't feel a thing.'

'Man, you don't get it: the pain is one thing, but I might not make the trip. I'm gone, I'm fucked. I only just made it through a twenty-minute taxi ride. What's a fourteen-hour bus trip going to be like?'

He could tell I wasn't well, and I know he wanted to get home as much as I did. I wanted to arrive in a plane seat, though, not stuffed in a coffin. The only other option I had was going back to the hospital, and that sure as hell wasn't going to happen. I nodded to Ruben, accepting the 14 hours of torture that was likely to come.

'Sweet, we are going home!' Ruben said, as he shoved stuff into his suitcase.

Tomorrow seemed so far away, yet Ruben's mood was infectious – I felt a lot better. I was tingling with excitement and a well-needed burst of energy. It didn't last long: as I laid my head down for sleep that night I had the ghastly realisation that after the 14-hour bus ride I still had to sit on a plane for another eight hours.

My leg was throbbing, but worse still was the miserable ache of the friction sore on my tail bone. It was bleeding, and the smell of the pus coming out of it made me feel ill.

I was in a bad way. My last night in Bangkok and I couldn't sleep. The whole trip kept playing over in my mind. *What if I had died in that accident?* I thought. *What would have happened? I wouldn't have woken up. Where would I be? I wouldn't even know I had died.* I was so drunk that I would have been robbed knowing of my own demise. *Where would I be now?*

What if I got busted with the drugs? I would be in a Thailand prison. My parents would have to come and see me locked away in a foreign country. I would have been on the news and totally destroyed my parents' lives.

I still didn't know if the effects of the broken condom would come back to haunt me. *What if I had HIV? Imagine what people would think?*

I didn't know if we were in the clear from the mob and getting home. *What if they get me? I will be killed!*

Will I still be allowed in the navy when I got home? What would I do about my situation with Anne? I'm going to live with her, but is it something I really want? What am I going to do about work?

My mind was on fire; there's no wonder I couldn't sleep.

Chapter 14

FIGHTING IS UNIVERSAL

Monday, 1 December

It was the first day of December, the day I normally spent putting up the family Christmas tree with Mum. I hoped I would get to see her again. Sleep still eluded me. Ruben woke and sprung out of bed; he was on a high. I was torn by mixed feelings: the excitement of heading home, the doubt about whether it would still happen, the fear of making it through and the dread of the pain that lay ahead.

'Let's do it!' Ruben said. He left me alone with my thoughts to go and check out.

The unknowns of the plane ride caused me distress. Qantas, the well-known Australian airline, had organised a mercy flight for people needing special care. Kids, the elderly and the disabled took priority. They had come to our aide and we were now hopefully heading back to Sydney, but I should have been recovering in a hospital bed, not trekking across Thailand. I was worried that the airport officials would refuse me access, the corpse on wheels. *What if I was deemed unfit to fly?*

Ruben returned to the room, having checked us out. He helped me into my wheelchair and wheeled me to the elevator. A new development: it was hard to move my arms. With a ding the elevator doors opened to reveal a lady leaning against the mirrored walls. We both smiled at each other.

'Hello, how are you?' I asked as Ruben pushed me in. She looked at me with no response.

'How are you?' I asked again.

'No English, no,' she said, in what sounded like an Italian accent. 'Sorry.' I smiled.

She looked European but I was an ignorant Australian, believing everyone knew English. She stood dead still and looked straight ahead. I followed her lead.

'Fuck, I hope we don't see that guy I had the fight with,' Ruben said.

'Shhh,' I replied. Even though this lady didn't know English my subconscious mind jumped in to tell him to stop with the bad language. I hated swearing in front of normal people.

'Fight, fight,' the lady said.

We both looked at her.

'Fight, you fight,' she extended, now looking angry.

With another ding of the bell we were at the bottom floor as she burst out the doors. I looked at Ruben.

'What the fuck?' he asked. He pushed me out of the lift and we headed for the exit.

'Hey!' someone shouted from behind. I looked around to see the man Ruben had gotten into the fight with standing with the lady from the lift. She didn't know English, which meant she couldn't understand when I asked how she was. It's sad to say the word 'fight', though, is universal.

The man bolted over at full speed. Ruben froze in shock for a second before shaping up to fight. The mustached man picked up pace as he closed the gap. With a loud crunching of bone on bone, he tackled Ruben to the tiled floor. They slid for 5 metres before stopping. Ruben was underneath the man, who from his heightened position threw a punch that landed hard on Ruben's forehead and bounced his head off the floor.

'Fucking get him, Ruben!' I screamed as I attempted to dash over in my wheelchair to back him up. Thoughts of my painful body disappeared. Adrenaline had kicked my arms into action. I could have been knocked to the ground with a breath, but I would always back up my brother.

* * *

As I watched Ruben fighting my mind flashed back to an incident that had happened years earlier. I was in the city one Saturday night, perched up on the Town Hall steps. It was around 4 am and most of my crew had gone home, so only the remaining party animals remained. Most of them were impressionable young guys. We didn't want the night to end.

A large group of men were standing nearby waiting for the night ride bus home. They kept looking over, and I felt a confrontation energy come over me. I kept chatting away to my boys, keeping an eye on the other group.

Two of the men walked over. I stood up off the sandstone ledge: I wasn't going to get caught off guard.

'Hey, you work where my friend works, bro,' one of them said to Brad, who stood to my right. Brad was one of the only staunch boys left with me.

Brad looked past the two and over at the crowd of people at a solidly built man with dreadlocks who was pacing back and forth. 'Yeah, I work with him.' Brad then glared at me with eyes that hinted we were in some trouble.

'Yeah, he said you keep staring him out and thinks you want to fight him,' one of the two suggested.

As if on cue, the rest of the group made their way over.

'You think you're a tough man, hey? Well, what about now?' the dreadlocked assassin said, as he closed in confidently with a whole bunch of big men behind him.

The crowd that had remained with us were younger guys, just out to drink but now caught up in what might potentially become a harsh situation.

In a quandary about what move to make next, I scanned the crowd. There were seven of them, all stretching their necks in an effort to make their already large frames look larger. All were looking for a fight.

I weighed them up against my boys. There were six of us, but only two standing. The younger four still sat on the bench: they weren't interested in backing us up.

Brad was the only other member of my crew, the only other one who would fight. *If only I had my real boys with me*, I thought, *not this bunch of young alcoholics.*

Exhibiting some judgement, I summed the situation up. 'Just have a one on one go, then,' I said to the now not so confident dreadlocked man.

This guy had obviously had the chance to have a go with Brad at work but didn't. I suspected he only had a heart when he outnumbered his competitor. Having a swarm of large friends gave him unjust confidence in his fighting ability. Outing him to have a one on one fight meant he was singled out, with no option but to take up the challenge. If he didn't have a go he was a coward.

This way I thought they could settle their differences by fighting toe to toe rather than having a brawl break out in which we were not only outnumbered but outmuscled.

'Yeah, bro, you got that shit,' one of our opponent's friends said, in turn accepting the deal.

That's all Brad had to hear, and he spat the lit cigarette from his mouth. Before the half-finished smoke's amber shattered on the floor, Brad threw a right hand that connected well. Hoping to avoid being hit again Dreadlocks ducked down, wrapped his arms around Brad's waist and speared him to the floor. The guy was strong. He managed to drive Brad into the ground even with Brad repeatedly punching him on top of the head, hoping for a reprieve in the tackle. Dreadlocks was now on top of Brad and throwing punches.

'Come on, Brad!' I yelled. Like a crocodile avoiding a poacher's ropes, Brad went into a death roll. He suddenly jolted, spinning off the concrete pavement, and reversed the position. He now had the advantage. He knelt on his enemy and kept punching as Dreadlocks flew all over the shop.

'Come on, cuz, get up!' I watched as this guy's friends got a little close to the fight, calling out for their boy to do better. I was pumped and my head bobbed up and down as though I was in a mosh pit, psyching myself up. 'Back the fuck off. Leave it, it's a one on one.' They hesitated. Reason seemed to sink in but for one guy.

He came from my left, his foot almost connecting with Brad's face. Luckily he missed.

This move was a dog's act and was the ignition for a brawl.

Reason left me as I ran over and grabbed hold of the dog who had kicked Brad with his paw. He started throwing shots at me with his head down, which gave me a perfect shot, so I gave him two uppercuts. 'That's it, Punchy, put him on show!' one of the younger boys from our group commentated from his seated position. I soon had the dog snoring on his back. He looked out of place on the pavement; he should have been in a kennel.

A punch to the back of my head changed my attention to someone else. I turned towards two men standing there shaping up, separating to come at me from different angles.

This wasn't going to be good.

'You want to mess with my brother?' I heard, as someone flew past and whacked one of them. It took me a second to realise it was Ruben. *Am I dreaming? Where did he come from?*

Ruben had been at a nearby nightclub drinking with some friends. He'd decided to leave, and on exiting was met by a girl commenting about a fight that had broken out close by. Ruben stood to watch before realising. 'Man, that's my brother!' He ran straight across like any brother would, and we were soon fighting back to back.

As if we were in a Hollywood movie, he reached us just in time. The fight didn't last for much longer after that.

Sirens blared from approaching police cars and the fight dispersed. I was left with my brother and a friend of his who had also backed us up. We were celebrating the circumstances as we called it a night and jumped into a taxi.

* * *

Now, in Thailand, it was my turn to back up my brother.

On my way to somehow helping Ruben managed to throw his own punch, connecting flush on the jaw of his opponent, which rocked him.

'Yes!' I hollered.

Ruben was now in control. He continued to throw punches until the shrieking of the lady from the lift cut in through his rage. She was speaking a foreign language, and I guessed she was asking for help.

Ruben climbed off the man; both were bleeding. He didn't wait, but pushed me hurriedly outside and launched us both into a taxi.

'Fuck,' Ruben said, pressing his shirt to the back of his bleeding head.

'You okay?' I asked.

'Yeah,' he said, tapping his lip and looking at his fingers to check for blood. 'Where the fuck did he come from?' he asked.

'It's 'cause that lady heard you say fight,' I explained.

'Why did I say that?' he moaned. 'I always put my foot in it. I've gotta learn to be quiet.'

Ding. Just . . . *Ding.* Be . . . *Ding.* Silent . . .

The taxi drove us to the meeting place of our bus departure – a hotel just on the outskirts of Bangkok. Ruben squirmed from the pains he had, though after cleaning himself up the wounds to his head weren't as bad as we originally thought. Head wounds always bleed heavily. I writhed in pain for the entire 10-minute ride. It was hell; my whole body was aching. I had little relief from the drugs I was taking as my body had built up a tolerance to the meds and they were no longer working.

A large crowd of people mingled around the meeting place. Baggage was scattered everywhere among the tired, confused tourists who were jostling for a position at the start of one of the many queues. At the head of these lines were clipboard-wielding officials who looked more stressed than the tourists were.

Everybody just wanted to get home and manners had been left back in hotel rooms.

From my position in the wheelchair I could subtly watch people without them noticing. I loved people watching, examining behaviour in different situations, and I now had the ultimate opportunity. I saw a mother drag her daughter, surely no older than four, straight to the front of a queue and slam down her suitcase. Whispers spread from the line and expressions shifted across the faces of those behind her: anger, disappointment, bemusement.

Watching their reactions took me back to a time when I had been around seven years old. I was with my aunt and we were lined up to get lunch at a food court when another lady pushed right in front of us. I felt my aunt's hand tighten around mine and I looked up to see her angry face. 'Excuse me!' she said, before pushing back in front of the lady. That should have been the end of it, but for the rest of the day I overheard my aunt telling people how angry it made her that people could be so selfish.

A few weeks later I was lining up at the school canteen when an older kid pushed in front of me. I snapped. 'What are you doing? I was here first.'

He turned around and simply said, 'Too bad.'

I stood angrily.

A friend I was with noticed my reaction. 'Who cares?' he said to me.

Mirroring my aunt's hatred towards selfishness, I replied: 'What do you mean? I was here first, he pushed in. You don't push in front of people. I hate selfish people.'

He continued. 'My dad told me that if people push in then they must be in a really important rush and it's not worth getting angry for. He said if people push in just smile and know that you're happy being where you are.'

After years of watching those around me react in anger, I was trained that anger was the way to behave when someone pushed into a line. My friend, on the other hand, had learned to smile.

Same event; opposite reactions.

A situation isn't the determining factor in a reaction; our interpretation of it is. How many bad days have you had because you took something the wrong way?

This situation in Thailand was obviously a terrible time that was filled with pain and fear, though it was still one of the luckiest things to have ever happened to me. I was riding a motorbike blind drunk with no helmet, smashed straight into a pickup truck and survived. Thailand is the number one tourist spot for Australians to die. I didn't. Getting released from hospital as well after Dad had managed to get cash was another bit of good fortune I didn't feel I deserved. My interpretation at the time was 'poor me' and that of a victim. My perception of the event now is that it's one of the best things that ever happened to me.

Same event; shifted perspective.

The mind's power is earth-shaking. Train it to be an advantage.

One of the officials approached the lady and said nicely, 'Sorry, but all these people have been lining up for the last twenty minutes. We have all your names on this list so you will still get on a bus. Please head to the back of the line.'

'I've been stuck in this damn country for over a week, I'm sick of it. We are getting on this bus,' she shot back.

'Miss, I already explained that we have your names down so you will get on a bus regardless,' the official tried to reason.

'We are getting on this one!'

A couple of ladies further down the queue had begun yelling. I turned around and saw one of them waving her fists about while she shouted. She stormed forward and glared right in the face of the mother. She looked ready to hit her with her tightly clenched fist.

'Get to the back of the line, you selfish bitch. We have all been stuck in this country and are all sick of it! Get to the back of the fucking line!' she shrieked. Another woman, likely a friend of the fist shaker, backed her up.

The mother stood staunch. 'No! How dare you talk to me like that!' Her daughter was crying and being pulled from side to side, caught in the fray. I sat watching it all unfold. An elderly man who was at the front of the line gently tapped the irritated lady on the arm. She stopped and turned, and the other ladies followed suit.

'You can take my spot if it's going to stop all this arguing.' He pulled the handle out of his suitcase and stepped out of the line. 'There you go.' He peacefully made his way to the back of the line, dragging his suitcase behind him.

Among the chaos some reason had emanated. Everyone stood silently to watch the unlikely peacemaker. The two ladies who had been arguing stood motionless, and the little girl had stopped crying. The fist shaker was voicelessly apologising, looking into everyone's eyes. She had been brought back to the moment and out of her enraged head. The chaos was over, and the ladies stood embarrassed as they quietly waited to get on the bus.

This event showcased every emotion and human trait imaginable. The lady who had pushed in was extremely selfish and impatient, the other angry and confrontational. The official had been diplomatic, reasonable and expectant of a positive outcome. The little girl had been anxious, crying, upset and frightened. The elderly man had been humble, patient and kind in his beautiful actions. The crowd had been disappointed. The arguing ladies also became embarrassed.

I was interested. Ruben was amused.

The outcome may have been different if the mother had understood the importance of a silent mind. She had simply jumped out of the taxi, glanced around at the endless queues and snapped. Whatever kindness, generosity and fairness might have existed in her was suffocated under rage and jealousy. With her mind screaming, she didn't have an opportunity to be reasonable.

After a half hour wait Ruben was assisted by a stranger to get me aboard a bus. There was no way I could have crutched my way up, since using the crutches was extremely tolling on my arms, bruising and scratching me every time I used them. It was easiest and fastest to have someone carry me up and this man was kind enough to help. My resemblance to a zombie didn't deter this kind man, while others kept away. Now on the bus, I made my way to an aisle seat and collapsed into it. Just being upright had become a burden.

'Bro, move over,' Ruben said.

'I told you before, I can't sit on the window seat. I can't bend my leg,' I whined, disappointed he had forgotten.

'Well, I can't climb over you.'

'Bro,' I sighed. I heaved myself up in annoyance to let Ruben through to the window seat. The whole affair held up the other passengers, who were piled in the aisle of the bus and waiting to land in their own seats.

Once Ruben was settled I had to consider my options for keeping my leg elevated. After some fidgeting my only option was to rest my leg on my bag, which I had thrown into the middle of the aisle. It wasn't elevated enough.

'Man, this isn't going to work,' I helplessly said as I turned to Ruben.

'What d'you mean? We are on our way home!'

'My leg isn't high enough. It's still lower than my hip and all the fluid has already run to it. Look!' I motioned for Ruben to look at my leg and he leaned across me. My swollen, purple, smelly, dirty leg stared back at him as if crying for help.

'We are on our way home,' was all he could say.

I was sure my leg was going to be amputated when we got home. I was weak – I couldn't eat and I was feeling sick. Had the infection spread? I started to imagine what life would be like back home as an amputee. How would I keep boxing? I wondered if boxing was an official sport in the Paralympics, but quickly forced that thought out of my head as the bus started up.

With a liberating release of the hand brake the bus was finally on the move. Despite the pain I felt a wave of relief wash over me. As the bus spat out fumes you could practically see all the tension being released out of the people onboard and into the air. It was like a big group sigh of relief. Everybody on the bus wanted to get back to Australia, and being in motion signalled that we were on our way home.

We drove through Bangkok and were soon on the outskirts of the city. Ruben had fallen asleep already and I looked past him through the window. Large billboards lined the sides of the highway. As we pulled out of the city I got a chance to see the beautiful countryside of Thailand. It was a nice distraction from my pain and thoughts of a possible amputation, but just half an hour in I became awfully irritated and anxious. My foot was shaped like a rugby ball with five toe nuggets hanging off the front. When I touched my leg my finger left a deep imprint in the flesh.

Fuck this trip. Everyone on this bus thinks they've got it bad. What about me? They've got no idea what I've been through.

I looked around at the other people on the bus and caught the eye of a Thai lady with a young boy resting on her. She smiled a beautiful warm smile at me that radiated with a wholesome energy. It felt as if my mum was giving me a hug. We looked at each other for a while. I was speechless. We both slowly looked away and I sat with a little grin on my face, thankful for her gesture.

One hour in my leg pain was increasing. My leg was swelling and I couldn't feel my toes. I kept shifting my weight from my left butt cheek to my right. If I sat straight on the deep wound of the friction sore it reminded me I had pain in other places too.

Only one hour down! I have another 13 of this. It's not going to be good, I thought.

The passengers had grown quiet. I watched as conversations stopped and people started to prepare themselves for the trip ahead. A lady pulled out a pillow; another took out a pair of eye shields and rested her head to sleep. I let my mind wander back to the Thai countryside, trying to focus more on the scenery and less on my pain. Ruben snored. I watched his sleeping face: he looked so innocent.

Thump!

A shock wave raced through my body. The bus had hit a bump in the road that took my breath away. I swore through my teeth and pleaded for the pain to subside. Ruben kept sleeping innocently.

Two hours down, 12 to go.

Time continued unerringly. Pain! I wanted to wake Ruben to convince him to tell the bus driver to stop and let us off. Lying on the side of the road seemed a better option than this painful ride. The chair was uncomfortable, and fluid constantly ran into my now throbbing leg. I just wanted to get off. The bus seemed to be shrinking and the air was becoming thicker as I struggled to breathe. *When I get home, I'm never leaving the country. I'm never drinking again and I will never ride a bike again. I'm sick of this shit happening to me! I didn't deserve this.* The self-pity was back!

Three hours down, 11 to go.

I dreaded every time somebody in front of us stood up, which usually meant they were going to the toilet. It was at the back of the bus and they had to climb over my leg to get to it. The first few times I was apologetic to those having to pass me but I soon grew tired of it, choosing instead to remain silent and look away. That worked well until one man made it halfway over. He was lifting his second leg over me when the bus shook, causing him to fall right on my leg.

'Ah, fuck!' I screamed in pain. 'Ah, my leg!' I continued through clenched teeth and a grimace.

'What happened?' Ruben's sleepy voice croaked.

'I'm so sorry,' the man said, regaining his feet.

'Are you kidding? Watch what you're doing!' I was curt, still thrashing with pain.

'I'm sorry,' he repeated before continuing to the toilet.

'He fell on my leg,' I said to Ruben, as he drifted back to sleep.

After that incident, whenever someone headed to the toilet my leg would tingle in pain as if readying itself for a second hit. This demonstrated again the power of the mind and how easily it is negatively conditioned. Ten people passed me without a problem and my leg just sat there relaxed, but that one time my leg was bumped caused me distress and formed the belief that a person rising was the precursor of pain. My leg would actually already feel pain as a person approached. Nothing had yet touched it, but my mind had connected the dots: person rising to go to the toilet equals pain. In reality, though, the pain happened one time out of 10; the other nine times it had been fine.

Our minds are so quick to associate with the negative and condition all our actions and body responses for this. We need to evaluate our thinking and current beliefs, the majority of which are formed by our exaggerated minds trying to convince us we need protecting. In life it's so much easier to think about pain and heartache as it is literally everywhere: news reports, depressed people on social media and even in everyday conversations you overhear on the street or when riding the bus. Living in a world where channel ratings score for drama but sink for positivity meant I spent most of my life bending to the will of society. When I found out something bad I wanted to be the first to tell everybody. Why? It's bad news, and usually someone else's. For some reason I just couldn't help myself.

When I heard bad news, spreading it was satisfying, perhaps because it sparked something in me. It changed my monotonous day and allowed me to feel something. I was often bored, living day to day with the same thoughts, same television, same depressing conversations, same working week and same weekends. Bad news changed that. The harsher it was the more remarkable, and for that short time I felt invigorated. I used to thrive on drama; my mind loved it. Eventually, I released the incessant bad thoughts and began living in the moment. I found myself detaching from the drama – the daily news, negative people – and my conversations were soon flowing with laughter and positivity. Boredom no longer has a place in my life. It has stopped existing, for I live in the present – the now.

We need to evaluate everything and separate from anything that isn't serving us. Look for good and you will find it everywhere.

While I was sitting on the bus I tried to focus on something that would take my mind off the pain: happy thoughts, things back home or anything that would make me feel better and focus less on the agony. Massages. Friends. Family. Good food that wasn't ice cream. I felt a little better before quickly bouncing back to the pain after the bus hit another bump in the road.

Four hours down, 10 to go. More excruciating pain!

Five hours down, nine to go.

Ruben was asleep again, and I envied him his ability to sleep anywhere. My mind was always too busy for an enforced sleep. My foot was so puffed up with fluid that it was now hard to move my toes. I had never felt so scared and uncomfortable.

Seven hours had passed and I was near tears, struggling with all the pain and worry. I was breathing heavily through anxiety, the anxiety was feeding the pain and the pain was feeding the anxiety: a perpetual cycle. A fucking nightmare. I was busting to use the toilet but couldn't imagine trying to get to the back of the bus without falling over, and the thought of falling over made my leg pulsate even more, warning me not to dare attempt it.

Eight hours down, six to go. We were closer to the end. The officials had advised us that we were scheduled to stop for a food break in an hour. Still busting to go to the loo, I hoped I could hold off until then. Swollen, bruised leg, fat feet, deep pain in my hip, a smelly friction sore on my tail bone and a full bladder – which one should I worry about more?

The bus started to slow. Thank God!

I craned my neck to see out the window past Ruben, who was still sleeping. The bus was pulling into a tourist stop that had a large restaurant with a souvenir shop. Ruben finally stirred.

'I really need your help here, bro.' The words fell out of my half-opened sticky mouth.

A man got up from behind me, straightened his shirt, walked down the aisle and stopped at my leg.

'Sorry, mate. You're going to have to jump over,' I apologised.

'Are you getting off?' he asked.

'Sure am, I'm dying to raise my leg.'

'Well, up you get.'

'Nah, I'll take a while. You guys go through first.'

'It's okay, we can all wait,' he said, as he placed his bag on the floor. 'I can help you up.'

'I can do it,' Ruben said, as he rose to his feet.

'Both of us can,' the man responded, pushing his glasses further up his nose. 'I'll grab under his right arm and you can do the same with his left.'

'I can do it, it's okay,' Ruben said, flexing his capabilities.

'Bro, it will be better if two people do it. I'm weak. I need the help,' I butted in.

Ruben looked at me for second then over at the man. 'Okay, then.'

I looked behind him at the rest of the people on the bus: everyone was okay with having to wait. Some sat back down and others stood and leaned on their seats, smiling at me as our eyes met. It seemed the tension from earlier when we had been boarding the bus had disappeared. Being told on numerous days we were heading home and then being told otherwise had left everyone feeling agitated.

When we try to control a situation our minds cause angst, and we feel we should be doing something to force an outcome. Now, seated on that bus, it finally felt as though we were actually on our way home. We didn't have to do anything.

'One, two, three and up!' the man said, his arm wrapped under me and Ruben assisting on the other side. Even though the pain was there it still made me feel good that I was being helped and that other people on the bus weren't pissed off at having to wait.

Can he smell my body odour? Your underarm is right near him, he's going to think you're a grub. What about my breath? I bet I smell.

They were always there, my worrying thoughts.

'Thanks, mate,' I said to the man as he helped me off the last step on the bus.

'It's okay. I can carry you to inside the shop,' he responded.

'I'm okay from here. I just needed to get off that bus. Thanks so much, though.'

'Easy done.'

He walked away and left a slight smile on my face. The smile was wiped off when I looked up and saw we were about 50 metres from the entrance.

'I can't crutch there, it's too far,' I said, exhausted.

Ruben stopped and looked back at me, a picture of disappointment.

'What can I do? I can't get your wheelchair, it's at the back of all the luggage. Shouldn't have told that guy to go. We could've both carried you.'

'He already helped. I didn't want to be a pain in the arse.'

'Come on, you can do it!' Ruben attempted to encourage me.

'I'm going to piss myself!' Getting off the bus and interacting with the man had erased the pressing need to pee, but remembering about it had me busting.

I attempted to block the peeing situation from my mind and started to move, but every smack of the crutches against the road was a firm reminder that my circumstance was desperate.

It took me about 10 minutes to reach the entrance as I had to stop to catch my breath several times on the way. I was panting uncontrollably, and it felt as though I had been doing stair sprints in preparation for a fight. Thinking about that made me sad, as I couldn't see myself ever being that fit again. Thoughts ran through my head. *I don't think I'll ever be in a boxing ring again. Will I get back on the drugs and alcohol when I get home?* I had nothing else to look forward to, so I guess it was inevitable.

I found an empty cubicle, and the porcelain seat was a welcome place to rest after the gruelling trip to get to it. After that one relief I found a grass patch outside and lay on my back with my leg raised. For the first time in over seven hours I was able to raise it properly and I hoped the feeling would return to my foot. Maybe the pain would fade or some of the swelling, a second relief I would readily welcome.

'What do you want to eat?' Ruben asked.

'I don't know, something soft. My jaw hurts enough just trying to talk, so something nice and soft,' I murmured.

Ruben returned with a sponge cake, which I was happy to try. I sat up and took two painful mouthfuls before giving up. It just hurt too much. I continued to lie down, and people milled around me. After several minutes I watched as they all started heading back to the bus. Ruben motioned for me to get up.

'Please, just five more minutes? I want my leg to go down a bit.'

'Alright, time to go,' one of the bus officials demanded as she walked past. There went my five minutes.

Ruben had to help me up. I slipped the crutches back under my armpits and took a breath to ready myself for the trek back to the bus. It felt like a marathon, with Ruben as my support team. The stop-start trip took what felt like 10 minutes. When we reached the bus we were greeted by people who were now visually annoyed at having to wait for us. I guess patience is limited.

As I hopped on I heard a man mutter under his breath, 'About time.' I stopped and glared at him, my face ablaze. Inside, I wanted to attack him, and I hoped my glare mirrored that. He looked up at me then sheepishly looked away.

I wasn't letting this pass, so whispered back, 'You piece of shit.'

Even in the sorry state I was in I still would have at least tried to tear his head off. The altercation had made me tense with anger, a heavy, painful anger. I loved it, because feeling that pain meant I forgot about the other. I slunk into my seat and revelled in it. The bus kicked into gear and we were off again.

Nine hours down, five to go.

As the sun set I began thinking about home, and a tear rolled down my cheek. I thought of Mum and Dad eating cheese on toast for dinner because they'd run out of money for the week. That was my fault. They had sent over 20,000 wasted dollars for me, and I knew how tough they had already been doing it. I sat on that bus in Thailand heartbroken.

Ten hours down, four to go. More tears.

Eleven hours down, three to go. Death felt a better option than having to deal with the last three hours.

The sun was just about gone and darkness had taken over the skies. Ruben, having fallen asleep again, snored loudly. Sleep still eluded me.

Thirteen hours down, one to go.

'The last hour,' I whispered to myself. It ticked by slowly. Resting people started to stir in their seats. The Thai lady who had smiled at me earlier was packing her child's toys away. She'd had them out to keep him occupied. A man in front of me took his earphones out and chatted to the lady next to him for the first time in 12 hours.

Each time the bus slowed my heart skipped a beat. I thought we had reached our destination, only to be disappointed when it sped up again. As the minutes ticked on so, too, did my worry. I was petrified I would die and arrive in Phuket a messy corpse, but there were now only minutes to go until I got off the bus of pain.

By the time we pulled into Phuket it was deep into the night and raining extremely hard. *The way things have been going,* I thought, *a storm would definitely be the catalyst for us remaining here another day or two.*

The bus slowed to a crawl as the driver navigated the streets. We were going through a quiet street when a cyclist cut in front of us, forcing the bus driver to slam on his breaks. We slid on the wet road, the cyclist scarpering out of the way just in time. We eventually came to a halt after what felt like an eternity. Ruben woke up.

'Man, are we there?' he said.

It took me a moment to respond. 'Yep, pretty much.'

'About fucking time,' he said, wiping the drool off his chin.

I just stared at him.

It took another five minutes to arrive at the airport. Ruben wasted no time. 'We don't need that guy to help.'

He practically scraped me from my seat, then I wrapped my arm around him and he carried me off the bus. I'm sure that everyone on the bus had the same idea of getting off quickly, though again their patience was back and they took their time. Once we were through the terminal doors we joined crowds of people rushing around aimlessly.

There was a frenetic energy about, everyone searching for what they should be doing and each wanting to be the first to find the answer.

Clipboard-holding officials were speaking to airport officials, who looked confused. I noticed a woman in clean-cut business clothes, different from all the tourists. She looked calm and prepared. I recognised her from somewhere but couldn't place her until I saw two men carrying a camera and tripod then setting the camera up to face her. Ah, that's who she was: a news reporter from Australia. It was incredibly soothing to see her because surely this meant we were heading home.

'Airlie Walsh here for Nine News in Phuket, Thailand,' she began her report.

'Kennedy!' we heard a different lady holler. Ruben pushed me towards her.

After returning home I found out that scores of friends and family in Australia witnessed me on television being pushed around in a wheelchair. I hadn't told many people I was going on the trip because it had been a split-second decision.

'I was sitting in the lounge room with my mum and brother watching the news and the first thing we see is you getting pushed in a wheelchair,' a friend later told me. 'I was like, what the fuck? There's Punchy in Thailand. He's in a fucking wheelchair. What's he done now?'

You can imagine everyone's surprise at seeing me there, not knowing I had even left the country let alone being pushed around in a wheelchair. It was just another story I had to tell.

'She called out Kennedy, yeah?' Ruben asked me.

'Yeah, I'm pretty sure.'

'Did you call out Kennedy?' Ruben asked, approaching the woman. We needed to be sure.

'Yes, sir,' she said, smiling at Ruben before looking down at me. Her smile faded when she saw the condition I was in.

I noticed this, and with all my energy I smiled and said loudly: 'Hello, there, how are you doing? I'm Luke, this is Ruben.'

'Umm,' was all she could manage.

I was hoping my energised greeting would persuade her I was okay to fly.

'We have good news,' she said, still looking at me with concern.

Yes! I thought. *It worked! Now please let that good news be that we are going home.*

'We have a flight leaving in one hour. Your seat is in business class, so you can keep your leg straight as you need to. It'll be like a bed.' The generous words slid out of her mouth elegantly and made me feel as though I could have done cartwheels back to Australia. Ruben had a big grin on his face.

As she turned back to Ruben the woman's voice dropped a tone. 'Sorry, sir, we could only get your brother in business class. You will have to sit in economy.' She walked away, leaving one of us a happy man.

'What? That's bullshit. Why can't they get you in business too?' The least I could do was act like I cared.

'Fuck it. I don't care,' he said.

My elation didn't last for long as the woman soon returned with some further news. 'I have some bad news.'

I looked up at her, trying to remain calm. Somehow I knew this had been coming. She seemed taken aback; maybe she was expecting me to blow up. I chose not to be angry. I had accepted this trip was doomed so I expected the cloud would lose its silver lining.

'We have to stop off in Singapore for twenty-four hours. We then cannot guarantee you a business class seat so you may have to wait there until we can get you an upgrade.'

'Aw, fuck,' Ruben replied.

I hated that he swore in front of her. Sure, we'd swear a heap, but this lady was only trying to help.

'At least we can get about halfway home,' I said to Ruben, trying to cheer him up. The lady looked at me a little confusedly.

'So how long is the flight?' My stupid ignorance shone through: I had no idea how far any country was from Australia. I thought the flight would get us at least halfway home and didn't realise that halfway home was actually over the Indian Ocean.

'Just under two hours,' she said.

I looked up at Ruben, who was clearly exasperated with my stupidity. He looked to the ceiling for support, his breath exiting in a long, slow sigh.

'Bro,' I fretted. 'We are flying to Singapore, it's not even a two-hour flight. It might be days before we get another flight from there.' Ruben didn't answer; he simply pushed me along to check in our bags.

The joy of knowing we were finally getting on a flight was clouded with worry. Once we landed in Singapore we didn't know how long it would take before I would be upgraded to business class again or *if* I would. I couldn't bend my leg, and I doubted that any airline would allow me to sit with my leg sticking out in the aisle. Flying economy was out of the question. To make things even worse, my mouth was starting to fill up with sores and I had no idea what from. The worry? Lack of good food? All the drugs?

I was falling to pieces.

I hadn't showered since the two nurses had washed me during my hospital stay 10 days ago. It was difficult to shower because I couldn't get my leg wet and I hadn't bothered to ask Ruben for his help. He wouldn't have done it. I did attempt to wash places I could reach after using the toilet occasionally. My skin was oily and smelly and I was sure it was aggravating my tail bone sore, which was now giving me more pain than my leg injury.

'Please come with me, Luke, it's time to board,' the bearer of the news said. She held on to the handles of my wheelchair and started to push.

'See you in Singapore, brother,' I hollered back at Ruben.

'Yep,' he replied.

'Here you go, Mr Kennedy. This lady's name is Lisa, she is a flight attendant. She will help you the rest of the way.' I was handed over like a baton in a relay.

I'd never flown business class before: it was an absolute dream. Lisa was beautiful. Her voice was soft and her perfume smelt fresh and natural like essential oils. She was gentle and made me feel as though she really cared. She took me to my seat, which was like a single sofa.

'Once we are in the air I can turn your seat into a bed,' she said, her voice sounding elegant. The seat was incredibly comfortable. It felt like marshmallow arms were coming out of it and giving me a big hug.

'Would you like a drink before we take off?' I wondered for a second if I should have a rum but opted for an orange juice instead. Lisa turned to walk away but I called her back as I had realised that the acid in the juice would cause stinging to the sores in my mouth. 'Sorry. No, I'll have a water.'

I watched Thailand shrink as the plane wheels left the ground. Not only was the land disappearing underneath me but so, too, was the threat of the mob getting us. We were safe at last from that torment.

For a few months after our trip I told this story with pride, speaking enthusiastically about how I got away from all my debtors. People's reactions would vary from bellowing laughter and teasing to quiet, fake smiles. I never really knew why: I mean, these people were trying to get money from me. 'Fuck them!' I used to say. I soon learned what those quiet, fake smiles meant. I had run from people who rightfully sought compensation from me.

I had done the wrong thing. At the time I firmly believed it wasn't that bad. I thought everyone was out to get me, and these people were just the same. I justified it by thinking the injured lady wasn't even injured, and I suppose I put the bike lady in the same bracket: they were just trying to do me over. I rarely took responsibility and always blamed others when something went wrong or if I messed up.

I knocked some guy out in a fight: his fault for talking shit.

I got caught cheating on Anne: wasn't me.

Late to work: the train came early and I missed it.

Said something that hurt a friend's feelings: had too much to drink.

I had been a drunk fool on a motorbike and had smashed it. These innocent people were just going about their day-to-day activities, and my narrow-minded and egotistical existence had affected their lives. I didn't see that at the time, though, but I do now. My selfishness caused an injury and loss of income for other people and both deserved compensation, however, I escaped this and now their trust in others would be lessened. My lack of empathy had a negative impact on their lives.

'You can go into the lying position now, sir.'

Lisa showed me how, and with a push of a button I was in my own cocoon with a screen in front of me. My upper torso was encased in its own little home. I searched the channels, expecting to come across the police chase again, but was surprised to flick to a channel playing *The Simpsons*. The ecstasy I felt at the memories that show brought me! I would normally be at home with my family, our dinner plates on our laps as we laughed at Homer's antics. I finally felt safe enough to sleep and didn't bother turning off the screen. I just buried myself into my marshmallow cocoon and settled down to drift off for what felt like the first time in years.

I'd barely shut my eyes when Lisa shook me awake. 'Mr Kennedy, we will be landing in five minutes. Please prepare by placing your seat up, sir.'

Chapter 15

SINGAPORE

Tuesday, 2 December; 6 am

I sat up and stretched as best I could to wake myself up properly. The plane was making its descent and I marvelled at the sun coming up over the horizon. *What does Singapore have in store for us?* I thought, as we touched the tarmac.

'Relax here, Mr Kennedy, until everyone gets off. Would you like another drink while you're waiting?' Lisa asked with her hand gently resting on my shoulder.

'No, thank you,' I smiled, loving her gentle touch.

'I'll be right back,' she said, before gracefully gliding away. She returned after a few minutes and helped me into the wheelchair she'd retrieved.

I exited the plane and searched around for Ruben.

'What does he look like?' Lisa asked.

'He —' Before I could explain Ruben announced his presence.

'Hey, fuck head,' I heard from my left.

'There he is,' I said to Lisa, as she smiled a fake smile.

'Good luck, Luke.' She touched my arm again and walked away.

I was back with Ruben, who'd already claimed our suitcases. He placed them on my lap and pushed me outside, where people queued for buses. Ruben wasn't chancing it and found a member of the support crew. I noticed she wore a name tag that read 'Susan'.

'Could we get the address for where we are staying? We are going to get a taxi.'

'Sir, the bus is for free. You will have to pay for a taxi.'

'That's okay, we don't want to wait. Anyways, he's in a bad state so I don't think another bus ride will be good for him.' He gestured to me to back up what he was saying.

She glanced over at me. 'I think he should be taken to the hospital.'

I smiled and pushed myself upright, hoping my depressed state wouldn't jeopardise our flight home.

'He's okay, we got checked just before we left,' Ruben lied.

It was my first time in Singapore, and I should have been excited. Instead I was severely depressed, and my head was so full of thoughts about death that I almost missed the country's beauty.

Ruben managed to get the address for our hotel, and we caught a taxi with little trouble. As we zipped along the streets I watched the city pass by. It was so clean: there was no rubbish anywhere, and an array of explosively coloured flowers lined the city streets. Huge plants and trees spanned the width of my vision. Buildings seemed to merge with plants, as though they were also growing from out of this garden. There was fresh greenery and bright, beautiful flowers everywhere. Gardeners were busy tending to most of the gardens, clipping, weeding and planting. These gardens were manicured, obviously tended to daily, which was proven by their intense charm.

Thirty minutes later we arrived at our hotel, where we were ushered inside by two local men wearing dark green uniforms. This place was crystal clean, and the lobby's ceiling was incredibly high. Nobody else from the mercy flight was there yet. Rather than wait both Ruben and I decided it would be best to sort our room out with the hotel now. We tentatively approached the counter but found that the transaction was quick and easy, and it was done without hassle. Our room was small, but I didn't care. I was happy to be lying on a bed with my leg elevated.

'I'm off,' Ruben said, after putting his suitcase down.

'Where're you going?'

'I don't know. I'm just going out.'

Ruben left. Alone again, I sat watching television. Again there was no sign of the police car chase, so this television was going to be good to me too. We still didn't know how long we were going to be in Singapore for. We had been notified that a flight was due to leave the next night but didn't know if that meant an upgrade and I would be let on it.

I wasn't alone long. A few hours passed then Ruben returned.

'Hey, we're flying home tomorrow. They got us on the flight.' He sat on the bed.

'Yes!' I was tearful with joy. 'We are going home.' I breathed in relief, then thoughts crept in of the trip ahead. I was dreading the nine-hour flight in a seated position. I had been lucky to make the 14-hour bus trip without dying. It felt as though Susan, the kind woman who'd helped us find this hotel, was ready to sign my death certificate after she had taken one look at me. I just wanted to get home and tried to hide my fear from Ruben, but my silence and the look on my face betrayed my attempt at composure.

'What's wrong with you? We are going home!' Ruben interrupted my thoughts.

'Yeah, sweet, can't wait,' I said to Ruben, as he smiled.

Ruben stayed in that night and we chatted a little before falling asleep. It felt good to have company.

Chapter 16

ANZAN

Wednesday, 3 December

Both of us woke up early the next morning.

'Let's grab some breakfast,' Ruben said.

As we made our way down the halls a large, orange-haired, freckle-faced Western man stopped when he noticed me.

He looked down at a folder, then at me. 'Are you Mr Kennedy?'

I didn't know whether to lie or confirm his question. Who was this guy?

'Yes,' Ruben answered for me.

'Great. I thought we'd lost you. We just went up to your room and no one was in,' the freckled man said. I noticed a kangaroo emblem stitched onto the pocket of his shirt, which meant he was a Qantas employee.

'We have a flight that leaves in three hours but we can't let you fly.'

My ears started to ring after he spoke and I couldn't hear anything else, even though he kept speaking. I was devastated and at my wit's end. This couldn't go on. He stood there with a funny look on his face, glancing at Ruben as though asking whether or not I had heard him. I snapped out of it to listen.

'You have to go to the hospital and get a DVT needle and then we can let you board.' His slower speaking pace and pronounced tone suggested he had repeated himself after failing to get a reaction out of me the first time.

'What's a DVT needle?' I asked.

'DVT is deep vein thrombosis,' he responded with doctor-like information. 'It is a blood clot that forms in a vein deep in the body. Blood clots occur when blood thickens and clumps together,' he continued. 'Most deep vein blood clots occur in the lower leg or thigh. They also can occur in other parts of the body. A blood clot in a deep vein can break off and travel through the bloodstream –' I drifted off, thinking about the flight '– cause death, Mr Kennedy.' That word brought me back. 'Blood clots in the thighs are more likely to break off, so because your whole leg, both thigh and lower, is affected by your injury you have a high risk of developing DVT.'

'Okay. Do any of your support team have the needle?' I asked.

'No, you are going to have to go to a local hospital,' he said with urgency.

Great! Another hospital.

'You better hurry. We are boarding in three hours,' he urged.

'Who's going to take us to the hospital?'

'Mr Kennedy, it's your responsibility to get the DVT needle so we can't supply transport. You are going to have to get a taxi,' Mr Freckles responded.

Qantas had supported us by providing the plane; now I just wished they had supplied a bus to the hospital. We were close to being out of money, and had to change Thai dollars to Singapore dollars at the hotel to get a taxi.

We wasted no time. Forgetting breakfast, we set out to locate the nearest hospital, which turned out to be 20 minutes away. We guessed that once we got there it would take another 30 minutes to get the DVT needle. The return 20-minute trip back to our hotel and the half hour trip to the airport totalled 1 hour 40 minutes, which would leave us with 20 minutes to spare. We would be cutting it fine.

With all the information we needed I barked: 'Let's go! We've got to get there quick, Ruben.'

'I'm not going.'

I laughed at his joke, but I stopped laughing quickly when I realised he hadn't joined in, nor was he smiling. He was serious: he wasn't going to go with me.

He saw the confused and shocked look on my face.

'Bro, I'm fucked. I can't go.' He looked down at me, his eyes pools of exhaustion.

He was wrecked. He'd had to push me all around a couple of different countries on top of all the partying, and he was done.

'You think you're fucked? What about me?' I said, playing the victim card.

'It's your fucking fault we're in this shit!' he shot out.

'Man, you're fucking –' I attempted before Ruben interrupted.

'Shut up for a second! You're always using bullshit excuses and getting out of shit. You fucked up, and all this is your fault. I've been wrecked too. I thought you were dead when I was told the news about your accident. Did you ever think how hard that was on me?' I just sat and listened. 'No! You didn't,' he continued. 'I've been going out and partying to get this shit off my mind. I thought you were dead, and when I found out you weren't all there's been is fucking drama with people trying to get money and shit. It's been the worst fucking week of my life.'

'Fair enough, man,' I said to him. 'I'm sorry.'

He was right. Okay, he was my brother and we back each other up always, but I had fucked up and it had affected him. I hadn't realised how much it had gotten to him emotionally. He had thought I was dead, and then there'd been nothing but bad news since. He was emotionally wrecked. The only way we knew how to handle our emotions was through drowning them with drugs, alcohol and sex. No wonder he was out partying: it was the only way he knew how to cope.

I wanted him to go with me to the hospital, but after getting out of my own head and observing him I could see he was spent. 'Go rest, bro. I'll be sweet.'

I was already on a tight schedule, and without Ruben's help it would get even tighter. Everything would be down to the second. I managed to wheel myself outside to wait for a taxi. It was only a minute before one pulled up, and I couldn't believe my luck. As I wheeled over toward it the driver took one look at me and rolled away. I guess he was in no mood to help a disabled person. Three minutes down.

Thankfully, another arrived in less than a minute and this driver wasted no time helping me into his taxi. 'One, two and lift,' he directed as he pulled me up from the chair and placed my arm around his neck. I was sure he had done this before.

'Thank you, thank you so much,' I said.

'No problem.' His reply was genuine. 'Where you going, sir?' he asked.

'To the hospital, please.'

'You don't look very good, I go fast.' He laughed a little.

'No, I'm okay, I just have to get some medicine for the plane home.'

We arrived at the hospital, a big, white, square building. The driver jumped out, grabbed my wheelchair and unfolded it outside my door, then manhandled me into it. He was very helpful.

'I will wait here for you,' he said, standing straight like a guard outside Buckingham Palace though with a smile on his face.

It was reassuring knowing this man would be waiting for me. I slowly pushed myself through the automatic doors – so slow, in fact, I thought they might close on me. I rolled up to the first counter I saw. At my seated height, all I could see was a woman's forehead.

'Excuse me. I need to see a doctor to get a DVT needle.'

'You need to see doctor, wait over there please,' the forehead said.

Her hand came over the counter to point across to people seated in a room. I wheeled myself over and waited with them. I noticed that everybody was seated quietly and waiting patiently. As names were called a smile would light one of their faces, indicating it had been their name that had been called. They would stand and be greeted by their doctor.

In Sydney hospital waiting rooms patience was almost non-existent. Most people would be waiting anxiously, shifting in their seats and muttering under their breaths. There could be arguments and fights. If somebody was called up earlier than others people would start yelling and swearing. People would complain that it wasn't fair because they had been there first even if the person who had been called was in need of more urgent help.

The positive energy in this room rubbed off on me and I sat waiting for my name to be called without stress. Even though I needed to be out of there quickly, somehow I knew to just relax and it would all be okay. I sat relaxed for half an hour, at peace, but it wasn't long before my mind's years of nervous experience kicked in. Twenty-three years of impatience was hard to break. At least I got half an hour of relaxation.

I began to get fidgety. *I need to leave,* my mind crept in to tease. *I need this needle now or I'm not going home.* It continued making me jittery. *I can't be stuck here again.* I looked around the room, my head flicking from side to side searching for answers. It was now over an hour into my schedule and time was ticking away. I kept looking around, hoping someone would notice my stressed face and make allowances for me to be seen more quickly. As I started pushing my impatient arse towards the counter my wheelchair became stuck. I felt something tug and drag me back a little, then turned and got a glimpse of an orange robe.

* * *

'Let me go, what are you . . .'

'Just be silent,' I heard in the easily recognisable voice of the Western monk from the temple. The only words I had heard him say when he stood at the bottom of the stairs in Thailand again shut me up for a second, and vibrated an energetic frequency through me.

'What do you want? Where have you –'

'Be silent,' he said, gently tapping my thigh as he sat cross-legged on the floor in front of me. 'It's how you have gotten yourself into this situation, you have –'

'What do you mean? How have I –' I cut him off.

This time he grabbed onto my thigh and a bolt of energy rushed through my body. Not the jolting, blood-rushing kind like when I felt anxious; no, this energy felt refreshing, like a comforting kiss from a loved one.

'I was talking and you cut me off. Just listen,' he said softly, his touch enforcing his words.

Okay, let's listen to what he has to say, I thought. *I mean, what have we got to lose? He seems like he can help. I wonder how long he's going to take, though. I need to get this needle. I feel . . .*

'Shhh, I just want you to listen to me.' He looked into my eyes.

'I didn't say anything,' I said defensively.

'How can you listen to what I'm saying through that loud mind?'

'How did you –' I stopped myself.

'That's better.' He smiled. 'My name is Anzan. So your mind doesn't come in to question things I want you to know that your name is being called in sixteen minutes. There is nothing you can do or say to speed that process up. No amount of frantic thoughts will help. Just sit here, peacefully.'

I instantly relaxed, my shoulders dropping a little as I sank into my wheelchair. I was normally agitated, thinking I could control situations, time or people. For instance, if Anne and I were going out I would storm around the house waiting impatiently for her to get ready. Standing over her while she brushed her hair was not an uncommon practice of mine: I was willing her to hurry up.

Why is she taking so long, it's like she fucking means it. Fuck this, I'm going now. No, you can't do that, she's driving. I'm about to yell, that will make her hurry up. Fuck this; she does it every time. I want to get out of here.

My mind would holler. The only time I would calm down was if the friends we were meeting rang to tell me they were going to be late. For some reason that was okay, I think because there was nothing I could do to make things go more quickly. Anne would have no idea what was going on in my head. 'Thanks, babe, you haven't rushed me tonight. Thanks for being so patient.' If only she knew.

Having direction about the duration I would have to wait made me feel good, somewhat in control. Hearing the monk sum things up for me was what I needed to shut my mouth as well as my thoughts.

'What I am about to tell you is so profound it will be the catalyst for you to set up your life from now and help you to understand a lot about incidences that have occurred and why.'

This should be good, I thought, doubting his words.

'Listen.' He released the grip he had on my thigh and placed his hands in his lap, then half-closed his eyes. 'One single thing is needed in your life to make it what you want it to be. Whether it's peace, abundance, happiness or love it can only be achieved through one thing.' He opened his eyes to look straight into mine. 'All you need is to be quiet.'

'That's all?' I asked, disappointed he wasn't giving me something groundbreaking.

'It's everything,' he said through a slow breath as he dimmed his eyes again, his mouth shifting into a smile. It seemed that what he had said was a part of him and what he was feeling looked as though it was pure bliss, like he didn't have nor ever had had a single worry.

'Mate, can you explain what you're saying so I understand? I don't go to church because I have no idea what's going on. Please just speak to me in plain English.'

'Let me show you,' he said, standing up. He reached forward with both hands and, like a psychic looking into a crystal ball, placed them above my head, his fingers spread wide. I felt weightless for a moment, then with a sudden jolt my head snapped forward like I was in a car crash. I regained my composure and looked up to see I was now standing inside a bedroom. It was dark but for a little light coming from a bedside table lamp. It flickered occasionally. Kneeling next to the bedside table was a lady with jet black hair, her elbows on the bed and her head resting on her clenched hands. She seemed to be muttering to herself.

I turned to Anzan, who was standing over her. I put my hands to my side and mouthed 'Where are we?' I didn't want the lady to know we had somehow broken into her house so I hoped Anzan could lip-read.

'She can't hear us,' he said, before turning slowly to look back down at her.

She lifted her head to reveal not only a tearful face but her identity. It was the motorbike lady, the lady who had gotten the mob together that I was hiding from for over a week. She was muttering to herself through tears, her lips bubbling a little with saliva.

'She's praying for something,' Anzan said.

'For what?' I asked.

'You.'

'Yeah, she wants to get her money. I bet she's praying the mob get me,' I said expectantly.

'What mob?'

'The mob she put together to get their money. I owe her and another lady money,' I said, like his had been a silly question.

'She's not praying for that,' Anzan said, raising his eyelids.

'You just said she's praying for me,' I responded rudely.

'She is praying for *you*.'

'See, you said it again. Make up your mind, mate.'

'Luke.' This time he spoke with authority. 'She's praying that you are okay and that you get home safely. She knows about the protests and knows you are suffering. She's praying, she's begging, and most importantly she's believing that you will make it home.'

I stood, speechless.

'That's what you need. Speechlessness,' he smirked.

'What about the mob?' I said slowly, feeling stupid as the words fell out of my mouth.

'That's an example right there.'

'Example of what?'

'Being quiet.'

'What do you mean?' I asked.

'I said I'd show you.' He placed his hands over my head again. After another snapping sensation I found myself standing in my hospital room in Pattaya. I looked over to the bed: there I was, sitting up with bandages covering my leg. I looked a sorry sight. I wanted to hug him. I wanted to hug me.

'Now you're tripping me out,' I said to Anzan. 'What's going on?'

'I wanted to go back a little and show you something. You asked where the mob was, and I'm going to show you.'

'How have we gone back in time? This is off its head. I must be having a trippy drug sleep,' I said. Anzan just looked at me. 'This isn't real,' I continued.

'Real?' he laughed. 'You live in your head anyway, how can you tell me what's real? Look,' he said, pointing back to the bed.

I looked over at my damaged self, who was sitting up and being fidgety. He started to feel around for something before he came into contact with the TV remote control.

'Here it comes.'

'What?' I asked.

'Watch him.' Anzan was referring to me. This was weird. With a push of the button the room lit up more as the television turned on. On the TV was the news report I had watched about a gang in Thailand killing people. Blood-soaked cushions were in a lounge room and there was a man face down on the floor next to them.

'Look at him. Look at you,' Anzan said.

I turned my attention from the TV and looked at my damaged self. His eyes were a little wider and he looked stiff.

'You see,' Anzan added.

'What?' I asked.

'That is where your mob is.'

'Where?' I looked around the room.

'The mob is not in the room; they're in there.' He slowly strolled over and stood in front of me.

'In where?' I asked, confused.

He leaned in further. His smooth bald head was the perfect top for his calm, round, unblemished face. Raising his robed arm slowly, he gently touched my forehead. 'They're in there.'

'Huh,' was all I could manage to say.

'Look again,' he said, pointing over to the bed. I looked over and saw my damaged self looking not only stiff but scared.

'You see that with being quiet there is no mob?'

I looked at him blankly. My thoughts rested. It was as though my soul knew that what I was about to learn was, indeed, life changing so it had shut my thoughts up.

'You were in bed recovering from your accident. The smash was a terrible thing to happen. That, too, could have been prevented with being quiet, but we will get to that soon.' He grinned a little. 'You see, Luke, you flicked on the news because you were bored.'

As he moved towards the bed, gently touching my past self, Anzan's face was a picture of sympathy.

'Boredom,' he continued, 'comes from the berserk mind always wanting to be fed: fed with stimulation, fed with noise. The news,' he sighed, 'it's always so loud with different segments telling us about war and poverty and crime. The bored mind loves it, and the worse the occasion the better. It feels more alive. It forgets about boredom when it is rabid. You also forget about your own pain.' He slowly nodded his head, as though agreeing with himself. 'Do you now see where the mob came from?' he asked.

'The news?' I answered, still not understanding him.

'In a way. Before watching the news the room was still. Your body was resting and your mind had a slight hush. Then your mind became bored and wanted feeding so it looked for noise. It found it on the news. The news then showed you a mob murdering people. This is where your mob came from.'

I shook my head a little as I began to understand.

'You see, Luke, if at that time the TV had shown stories of happy Thai people with their big smiles it is likely the

initial negativity would never have been impressed upon you.'
He stopped after noticing me drifting off a little. I'd do this if
stories were boring or if I didn't fully understand what I was
being told.

'Luke: do you understand what I'm saying?'

'I made the mob up?'

He simply nodded his head.

I thought back to all the times I'd watched the news with Dad.
During the harshest time in my life I would be drenched with fear,
believing the world was going to end because the news seemed
to tell me so. I couldn't recall ever hearing anything positive
from the news announcers; it was all about the pain the world
was suffering. I wondered if it was because things were actually
getting worse or just because I watched the news. I would turn on
the television and it would scream bloody murder. While flicking
channels I would be presented with an advertisement promoting
the reduction of heart disease risk via some product that probably
didn't work the way they were claiming.

I would be worried by everything I saw. To avoid it I'd pick
up my phone and trawl through social media in an attempt
to lift my spirits, but what I found were complaints: people
whining about witnessing a fight or that someone had stolen
from them. My next bet was to call a friend to meet for lunch,
but over lunch my friend would report the same news I had just
tried to avoid. They'd exaggerate the story then lace that with
more bad news. My entire surroundings were being raided by
bad news and negativity, a surety that I was hinged on fear and
anxiety, and now my mind was joining the race. It was making

things up to justify the belief that the world was out to get me.

If I don't watch bad news does it exist?

'Your thoughts set up your whole life. If you are being overstimulated by negativity your mind will be cruel. If your mind is cruel you can be sure your surrounding environment isn't going to be comfortable. I'm sure you don't want that sort of life.'

'You're right, but I don't really know what I want out of life.' I shook my head, as if disappointed at myself. I was attempting to show Anzan that I cared because, no doubt, he knew what life meant for him. I often felt compelled to mirror anyone I was speaking with, agreeing with what they said or pretending to have the same beliefs. I think it's because I worried about what they thought and wanted them to like me. I want everyone to like me. Did I like myself, though?

'You don't know what you want out of life because you are asking it with your mind. Luke, let me explain something further, and some of this may sound contradicting to the mind but just listen.'

I felt my pinpoint focus leave my mind, and it spread inside my body for its whole length and tingled.

'That is where you need to listen from.' Anzan noticed my shift. 'You see, this wisdom is to be felt, to be contemplated.'

'Isn't contemplation the same as thinking?' I asked, hoping that I had caught him out. The jump from body back up to mind was a quick one.

'Go back down to your heart,' he instructed. 'Contemplation is meditating, praying, observing and, okay, some thinking.'

He said 'some thinking' with a smirk, knowing I would have liked that. 'It's also art, creativity and analysing but with a soft focus. You sit relaxed and in the heart with something to contemplate, then you allow the topic to be put inside a feather. That feather slowly caresses the length of your body. Each time the soft edges touch your skin a drop of the new realisation leaves the feather and enters your awareness.'

'Where do the messages come from?' I asked.

'Where do you believe they come from?'

'God?'

'Good answer.' He smiled. 'Look, I don't know everything, but what I will say is these messages and feelings won't all be pleasurable. Some things that come up for you during these times of stillness can be tough to feel. It is another reason why you don't allow yourself to sit still, as it's often to avoid feeling what's deep within so you distract yourself.'

'I don't think that's right,' I butted in like I'd often do if I thought the person was wrong. 'There's not much I can't handle. I've been through a lot in my life and I'm still here. I'm a happy man.'

'Are you?'

When he asked that I felt my throat croak a little as though I was about to cry. 'Yes,' I said, this time forcing a smile.

'You are happy, but did you see what happened there? Your body has an intelligence that the mind cannot understand. Your body went to cry. Some deep emotions were hit by my direct question, and your body is what gave me the true answer. You then tried to hide it in a smile. Your smiles and laughs may often be genuine, however, a lot of the time they're to overtake or distract you from feeling what is really down there.'

'What's down there?'

'You tell me,' he said, knowing I knew the answer.

'Don't know.'

'You do know, but you're never still or silent enough to feel it.'

I took a deep breath.

'There you go,' he said.

'There's some pain,' I said, as Anzan closed his eyes. 'There's regret. Shame. Guilt. I've hurt people. I've seen people die. There's been a lot happen,' I said as a tear stroked my cheek.

'And you never felt any of it. That is what's below the smiles.'

'Why would I want to feel all of that, though?' I said as I wiped the tear away. 'I don't want to feel like shit.'

'Luke, those feelings and emotions deep down are what are preventing you from your truth. It is what is blocking the opposite flowing: your love, happiness and joy.'

'I do feel those. I'm always laughing and happy.'

'There's a difference between laughing at something funny and that of feeling unfettered joy. Look, at the moment you're hearing only words and your mind is trying to compare and make sense of it all. Allow this wisdom to sit with you and your soul will feel it. Don't push; let it be.'

'Is that where I find what I want in life?'

'You won't find what you want out of life, but if you're still enough it will find you.'

Anzan suddenly started laughing before gaining his composure. 'What's so funny?' I asked.

'Remember that I said I'd show you how you could have prevented the motorbike accident with silence?'

'Yes, but what does that have to do with knowing what I want in life?'

'You're making my job very easy. I have the same answer for both. Let's go,' he said, looking over at my damaged self on the bed. I glanced over too.

There I was, still restlessly fidgeting.

With another snap of my head I came to in an airport lobby.

'What are we doing here?' I asked Anzan, who was walking in front of me. I suddenly realised I was walking too. I had no pain; my leg was healed. 'I'm dreaming,' I said.

'We all are.' Anzan led me outside to daylight. 'That's why we are here,' he said, pointing over to a car pulling up at the curb. It was Dad's car, and it stopped directly in front of us and out jumped me and Ruben.

'This is us leaving for the trip last week. Why are you showing me this?' I kept my eyes on the car.

'Follow me,' Anzan said, walking closely behind Ruben and my past self, who were now entering the airport. I watched as Ruben pushed me away, laughing. They looked excited: if only they knew what was ahead.

They lined up quietly and waited to put their luggage through. They stood there glancing around the airport. My past self noticed a good-looking girl walk past so he grabbed Ruben and with a nod of his head pointed in the direction of the girl. Ruben looked over and flashed his eyebrows, implying that he, too, thought she was pretty.

'Why are we watching this? I mean, I've seen this shit before, this is –' Anzan placed his finger over his lips, which hushed me instantly.

Hope the trip is going to be good. Ruben will show me heaps. It's going to be fun. Can't wait to get drunk. Fuck, did I leave anything at home? Shouldn't have brought my mouthguard. Yeah, you should have, we will train over there. You're not going to train. Yeah. I will. See what happens.

Wonder how long the flight is? Can't wait for a drink. Think I need to go to the toilet. Nah, I can hold it. Probably not, where is the toilet?

Hearing this echo throughout the airport sounded like someone was playing a recording over the speaker, but it was my voice.

Should I have come on this trip? Of course, it's going to be the best! You think? Yeah, for sure!

Okay, see what happens. Where's that toilet? Hope this line hurries up. Imagine if we miss our flight; that would be fucked. Shit start to the trip.

And it continued, and continued.

'What is that? What's going on?' My head hurt. 'Where is it coming from?'

'Him.' Anzan pointed over at past me.

'He's not saying anything. It can't be coming from him.'

'It is.'

'Man, I'm looking right at him, his fucking lips aren't moving.' Anzan frowned, his lips pursed. 'Sorry. Sorry for swearing but, mate, you're telling me lies,' I shouted over the echoing voice continuing in the background.

Anzan spoke softly. 'Listen, and look at his mouth.'

What if the plane crashed? Now that would be fucked up. It would be so scary going down, imagine people's faces as we dropped to the ground. I hope I'd survive. Imagine surviving a plane crash: everyone would think you were superhuman. That would be crazy.

What about a terrorist attack? If a guy tried to take hijack the plane I'd knock him the fuck out. Now that would be good, I'd be a hero.

It just didn't stop.

'See, his mouth isn't moving.'

'Luke, I can see his mouth isn't moving. It's still coming from him, though.'

'Are you going to start making sense or just keep up with this speaking in code bullshit?'

He sighed. 'That noise, that echoing, shrieking, incessant arguing.'

'Yeah?'

'That's his thoughts. That's *your* thoughts.'

'My thoughts?'

'Yes. Do you not see? Are you not aware?' Anzan put his hand on my shoulder after noticing my worried face.

'Aware of what?'

'Life.'

I wasn't so sure I understood, so I kept watching.

Ruben and past me checked their luggage in, left the line and headed for the bar.

Can't wait for this drink. What should we have? A shot?

Nah, fuck that. Get it mixed with cola.

I'll have a couple of shots.

Nah, just get it mixed.

It's going to be expensive. The airport is a rip-off. They always lift the price on everything at the airport. Why do they do that? I'll shout Ruben a drink.

Nah, let him shout.

I'll buy the first one and he can grab the second. What if we don't have two, though?

Then he will owe me one.

The drumming voices continued as we walked behind them. I looked over at Anzan and shook my head, embarrassed.

'Don't be down,' he said.

'Of course I'm down, I'm fucking cuckoo,' I shot back.

'That must mean everyone is at some stage cuckoo.'

'What do you mean?'

'We all have these thoughts. Some more than others.'

'Even you?'

'In the past, yes. Watch!' he said urgently. 'This is why we are here. This is the answer to your accident as well as the answer to what you want in life.' He looked over as Ruben and my past self sat down.

'I'll have a rum and he'll have a beer,' I ordered at the bar.

'What kind of beer?' the bartender giggled along with Ruben.

I wasn't experienced in ordering beer. I always drank spirits, as did my friends; few of us drank beer. Ruben directed the bartender, 'Corona with lime, thanks.'

They think I'm an idiot, fuck that bartender. Laugh at me, the prick. Anyways, can't wait for my rum. Watch him. Make sure he pours a full shot, rip-off bastard. Ah, here it comes, my rum. It better be cold; I love a cold drink. This is going to be good.

His roaring mind continued as he grabbed the glass. I looked over at Anzan and shook my head.

'Pay attention or you will miss it. This is the moment.'

I looked back over. My past self lifted the glass towards his mouth, the berserk noise still screaming away. Then, with his first taste of rum . . .

Peace. Bliss.

'There's your answer.'

It was like the moment a neighbour stops mowing their lawn: replacing the annoying noise was a serene, refreshing silence.

I watched my past self sitting with one arm dangling by his side, the other resting on the bar with the drink in hand. His face looked different, as did his body. He looked relaxed.

'What happened?'

'What you just witnessed is the answer to your question, and your life.'

I watched Anzan's mouth move slowly. He spoke words that didn't seem to come from him. The sentence he'd said came from somewhere deep, somewhere even beyond the majestic Anzan.

'Alcohol is the answer?' I asked, with a smirk on my face.

'Now isn't the time to allow silly thoughts to enter. The answer comes down to one word, but let me explain something first.' He grabbed my hands and sat me down at a table, and while sitting across from me his grip on my hands remained although his touch felt soft.

'When we are born we are pure, like a clean white canvas. Initially free from thoughts, our mind is clear. There is an innocence so untouched that no word has the capability to explain it.' He closed his eyes and continued.

'We take on different labels and beliefs as we grow. We hear opinions and suggestions. Any incident that may occur to a child will have lasting effects throughout its entire life. Like a sponge, a child soaks up other people's realities. The blank canvas of life is painted on by another's brush. The purity of a relaxed, clear mind is tainted with concern for what other people's tarnished canvasses read. Worrying about what other people think compounds the anxious mind.

'"Imagine what they're going to think about us now," a parent might say. It is all it takes for a toddler to start their life with the capacity for embarrassment or guilt. A child could have their entire creative ability demolished if they are mocked for something as innocent as painting a picture. The child could develop a fear association with it and never attempt anything remotely creative again.' Anzan slowly shook his head as if remembering examples of what he was saying.

I stood and nodded my head.

'Luke, all of your beliefs in life come from hearing other people when you were younger: parents, teachers, neighbours and television.'

He sat still with his eyes closed. 'You live in your mind. Your mind is very loud,' he continued. 'It's stopping who you really are. The noise is smothering you.'

'Who am I?' I butted in. It was more of a plea than a question.

Anzan opened his eyes and gave me a little smile. 'You are pure, complete bliss. Ultimate happiness. I could use endless beautiful words and still not be able to fully explain it.'

'What is this single word, then, that sums up what I want out of life and also created the accident?' I asked.

'What happened when your past self took a sip of the drink?'

'He was relaxed?' I said, shrugging my shoulders, not fully understanding.

'Why was he relaxed?' Anzan asked.

'He was a little drunk?' I shot back.

'Luke, why do you drink alcohol?' Anzan asked, firmly.

'It feels good, it relaxes me. I forget about all my troubles.'

'Ah, there it is.' Anzan pointed his finger at me.

'What? I forget things? Is that what life is about?' I laughed a little.

'The one thing you were seeking that caused your accident. The same thing that we are all looking for without even knowing it.' He stopped and closed his eyes again. 'That one thing is ... silence.'

'That's it?' I said, my eyebrows raised.

'Of course your mind would wonder that, because with silence your frantic mind doesn't exist. You see, Luke, we all know what we want. Our minds hide it and our minds are also the reason for our wanting it. Like I said, we are born pure, we are free, then noise surrounds us and our true selves are imprisoned. What we are all reaching for is to be back to our pure state.'

He opened his eyes again, probably to see if I was listening. 'When your past self had a sip of that drink it lessened his thoughts. It gave him silence. That is why you drink, but alcohol doesn't take you back towards your pure state. It only intoxicates your thoughts; it hides them for a few moments. In the end, though, drinking does the opposite of what you are looking for. It takes you even further away from purity.

'Those brief moments of silence aren't worth the lifetime of depression, regret, pain and anxiety caused by the alcohol. Can you see how you're searching for something in these external sources? Can you now see what it is you're searching for and why?' Anzan asked.

'I think so.'

'You are searching for you. You are searching for peace.'

'Okay, I think get that, but what I don't get is . . . I mean, I have to use my mind to do stuff. If there was no mind I wouldn't be able to do anything. I'd love to travel, make money, have fun, spend time with friends: all that kind of stuff. The mind is a great tool! Does that make sense?'

'It does, though let me explain. Your mind is indeed a very powerful tool when it is used correctly, but for it to be used correctly it has to first be still.'

'See, now that doesn't make sense to me.' I was confused.

'Let me explain about tools and their benefits, and also where these tools fall apart. Let's look at time: why does it slow when we don't like what we're doing or when we want it to speed up? Why does it go so fast when we are sitting with people we really like? Eternity feels like seconds, and you could do it eternally.

'Time is a mind-made concept, an illusion even. An illusion. It's obviously a needed and beneficial tool for society to function but, like other great tools such as mobile phones, the mind's urge for stimulation has resulted in us becoming a slave to the tool, and the detrimental attachment and impact on mental health has now outweighed the benefits of these tools. When bored or doing an act you aren't happy doing your mind stirs and creeps in to meet the mind-made illusion of time, which causes time to solidify, to manifest as something that is "real". Thus the painstaking slowness of time.

'When you are relaxing with someone you're interested in, performing a passion or being creative your mind takes a back seat, as does the mind-made illusion of time. This is where your soul is revealed. This is where life is: free of mind-made angst. There's no such thing as yesterday, tomorrow or even a minute from now. They're all a mind-made concept, a concept that causes regret, fear, anxiety, depression, guilt, doubt and social awkwardness.

'We need a clock for our physical beings to function. We need presence for our souls to thrive. Physical is fleeting; soul is eternal. Make soul a priority. The addiction to mind has become a disease, and it's only getting worse.

'Luke, real happiness, real creativity, real love, real life come from stillness. Noise blocks this. You said you wanted to make money, which is fine, but to make the kind of money you want, honestly, you need ideas, inspiring ideas. They don't come from thought, they come from beyond thought, which is why it's important for your mind to be still.

'Happiness, the most breathtaking laughter and the biggest smiles all come when you are in the moment, away from thought and away from anxieties. I don't expect you to fully understand what I'm saying here. Just be still and listen. Your mind won't want to understand. I'm speaking to the pure you; he will feel what I'm saying.'

'Anzan, I just want to be happy,' I blurted out.

He smiled as though he had made a breakthrough. 'Luke, that is what we all want. That is who we are when we come into this world: pure happiness. We have just drifted far away from it with the noise of this world. Avoid news reports and negative people and be open to actually seeing what's in front of you, which is generally nothing. Nothing but now, which is everything.' Anzan took a deep breath.

'The last thing I want you to do is stress about this,' he continued. 'You will notice your thoughts more now, but don't be angry about them. They will lessen. Just get through and smile because you are aware.'

'How do I stop all the noise?' I asked.

'Luke, I could give you some great tools to help you. I'll start not with what you need to do but what you need to undo.'

'Huh?'

'When looking to change their lives people start chucking a bunch of new-age practices at themselves and it ends up just being more of a distraction. I will mention a few that help in a second but first, instead of learning, we need to unlearn. Our greatest advancements in life come not from learning but in the unlearning of our knowledge and beliefs and detaching from the things that aren't serving us.'

As I continued to stare at Anzan I felt my body totally relax.

'I suggest becoming conscious of how you feel, becoming present in your body and seeing what impacts you after hanging out with certain people. How do you feel? Do they bring you up, do you feel happy, supported, loved and energised?

'After leaving them, how do you feel? Do you feel drained and left worrying that what you told them in confidence they will tell other people? Are they negative? Were they judging others while you were with them, which made you feel like you were judged? Can you have a couple of hours' chat with them but later they crane one sentence out of it that you may have said and use it against you? How do you feel?

'After watching certain TV shows, how do you feel?

'After eating certain foods, how do you feel?

'After reading certain books, how do you feel?

'Break down every area of your life and see what's impacting it, then make some changes.'

'Okay, I get it, but some people who I love are negative. What do I do there? I don't want to leave them.'

'I get it. Thanks for that input. Some people we can't or don't want to separate from. Some are family, others co-workers. I get that, but we may have to watch our conversations around these people. Often, bringing to their attention how negative they are may make them realise. Start having some tough conversations with people. Bringing it to their awareness may bring about change. Taking responsibility, though: turn it back on yourself first because maybe you're the pain in the butt. Possibly you're the negative one. Have a look at yourself first.

'So, identify first what you may have to unlearn then chuck the other stuff in to help. I could say you need to do breath work daily, as this will indeed take you to who you are. I could ask you to read a lot, as this too will lead you towards silence. I could tell you to spend time with loved ones, as bringing you into the moment will lessen your worries and noise.

'Gratitude is another lovable aspect to silence. Being grateful for what you have brings you into alignment with who you are. This energy is one of the highest you could have for there is no need to search elsewhere for the things that make you feel good.

'Exercise: this too will help. It's why you like your boxing. There's stillness when you're in that ring.'

'Stillness?' I asked, knowing the only time someone was still in boxing was when they were knocked out.

'Stillness . . . of the mind. Any form of exercise gets you out of your head and into your body.'

'Is the stillness stuff from Buddhism? I don't want to be all religious.'

'Buddhism?'

'Yes, aren't you a Buddhist?'

Anzan started chuckling. 'No, no I'm not. I'm just me.'

'But look at what you're wearing. You were at the Buddhist temple.'

'I wasn't there for Buddhism; I was there for this. This is what I was there for.'

'What?'

'I was there for you.'

'Why?'

'Why not?'

'Here you go with all the cryptic stuff. This is why I don't go to church: all this cryptic stuff.'

'You don't go to church because you have to be still. You don't go to church because it brings things up inside of you that you don't want to feel. You don't go to church because your mind tries to make sense of it all.'

'You're saying I should go?'

'That is up to you. Church helped me a lot.'

'Now I'm even more confused. You look Buddhist, so you can't go to church.'

'Because I dress this way I can't believe? Luke, we are getting away from the point. I could tell you to seek happiness. Look for the beautiful things in life and lessen the external noise as much as possible. There will be a gradual shift away from the inner noise. You will reach your nirvana.

'All of these tools will help, but number one, which is a contradiction and one of the toughest: do none of the above. Stop looking outwards and go back into you and hear all the noise. Feel all the noise. Sit still and be tossed around and torn apart by what comes up: the emotions, pain, memories and feelings inside you, the things you've been hiding from. When you face it head on it's hard. It can be very challenging, and that's why people will get a taste of it and turn and run. They run away their entire lives from the diamonds waiting to be revealed if they're just brave enough to swim through the darkness and reach their demons head on. The demons transmute to diamonds.

'Stay with the darkness. Stare at it. Feel it. You'll then receive answers that are hidden behind the shadow you've been escaping from your entire life. This is what will bring you the most stillness, the most presence, the real love and joy. The darkness is hidden in there anyway, and it comes out into your real life in different ways. So why not face it to reveal it? Reveal it to understand it. Understanding it will show you what it is: a shadow, one that can transmute to light once understood.

'Do you remember your friend Kane when he elbowed that young lady?'

'How do you know about Kane?'

'The world that you know with its time and space restrictions isn't the one I experience. Anyway, that's not what I'm getting at here. Your friend Kane in his split moment of anger crushed the lady's jaw and his freedom. That's the result of not facing what's inside. He lost his mum when he was younger and had a lot of guilt behind it. These things may not have been thought about or felt for a long time, but they were bubbling up deep down. These deep shadows can manifest into many different emotions and actions, usually anger. That's what happened.'

I recalled all of the times I was angry and would lash out at people, only to regret it not long after.

'Luke.' Anzan noticed my overactive mind trying to make sense of everything again. 'Luke, I could tell you to look into these and a lot more and they might help, but that was my path. This is yours. The best advice I can give you is be aware, and you will find it yourself. It won't be an instant thing. Just know that the seed will be planted once you are aware. Only then can you just be.'

My mind didn't understand.

But I did.

* * *

Someone called my name.

'Luke Kennedy.'

I felt as though I was waking from a deep sleep and I looked up to see a lady in her early 40s who was wearing a white coat. The doctor. I smiled. I was in the hospital waiting room; Anzan was nowhere to be seen. Perhaps he was visiting another person's dream.

The doctor smiled back as I made my way towards her. Seeing me struggling, she met me halfway and began pushing me through an open door.

'Mr Kennedy, what happened to you?' She didn't wait for my answer. 'One moment, I'll get the nurse. You have to get into a bed. Your pallor is concerning.' She was calm and spoke assertively.

'I'm okay,' I said defensively. 'Seriously, I'm fine. I just have to get home.'

She heard the desperation in my voice and read it on my face. 'Okay. How can I help you then, Mr Kennedy?'

I explained my predicament.

'Yes, we can help you with that. I'll be back soon.'

While I waited for her return I noticed a photo of what appeared to be her family on one of the walls. The people had bright white smiles stretching from ear to ear.

As she re-entered the room she said, 'They are why I'm here.'

'Your family?'

'Yes. I love what I do, however, the hours are very long. When I get tired or frustrated I come in here and close the door. I look up at their faces and sit quietly for about five minutes. My frustration lessens and then I'm free. This helps me to remember that if not for this job I could not provide for them. They make me grateful for my position. I smile at them smiling at me.'

Maybe this gratitude thing does work.

Speaking about her family made me miss mine even more. I just wanted to hug my parents.

I just wanted to be home.

'Here you go.' She handed me a packet with a syringe in it.

'Don't you do it?' I asked, completely shocked.

'Sorry, sir, I didn't mention you have to do it just before you fly.'

'I have to inject myself?'

'Correct. Pinch this spot on your belly –' she showed me the rough position on her own body '– and inject. Don't get muscle and not near your belly button.'

I couldn't believe it. I didn't think I could inject myself but I took the needle anyway. I couldn't afford to fret; I was on the clock. My good friend the taxi driver was waiting for me with a big smile and he helped me into the car.

'We have to hurry,' I said. I wasn't sure he had heard me until the screeching of the tyres as we darted off indicated that he had. My mind was racing as fast as the car was.

Ruben better be ready! I thought, as the taxi flew around a corner and almost clipped another car. I kept looking at the needle. *I don't want to inject myself.*

We were driving on a straight road and my taxi friend pushed the car to its limits as its engine roared, giving my anxiety even more of a boost.

Just breathe.

I stopped looking out and ahead and turned to my breath. When I did that I realised how shallow my breaths were, and realising this I took deep breaths to fill myself up with oxygen. This instantly lessened my anxiety.

This shit actually works . . .

Can't wait to see Mum and Dad.

I held back tears as the car bounced up the driveway of our hotel before coming to a violent halt.

'Good luck, sir,' the driver said.

I pushed myself into the lobby and found the man who had told me to get the DVT shot.

I showed him the medical certificate he had requested and also the DVT needle.

'Cutting it fine, Mr Kennedy,' was his response. 'We have to leave in ten minutes.'

We had depleted our cash pool down to the last $50, so we had to take the bus this time.

'You get the needle?' Ruben asked. He had been sitting on a couch in the lobby.

'Yeah, I got it,' I replied. 'Ruben, I seriously need you to push me. I'm not doing too good, bro.'

'Yeah, okay. Sorry for before,' he replied, as he looked at me sympathetically.

'It's okay. I understand, bro. This way,' I said to him.

'Thanks,' he said, as he rose slowly from his seat and took the handles of my wheelchair. 'Man, I'm tired,' he added.

We got on the first bus we saw.

'Motorbike accident?' I heard in a deep Irish accent.

Two ladies were looking at me, so I nodded my head in agreement with their question. 'Yep, sure was,' I smiled.

'We knew it. There's so many over there.'

I felt like an idiot: I was a statistic. Another fucking stupid foreigner who thought they were invincible.

For the entire bus ride I dreaded the flight. I was worried about sitting on my infected tail bone for the duration and didn't know how I was going to cope. *Just get me on that plane; I want to get home,* I thought.

The plane was due to leave in just over an hour.

We are heading home! That thought alone lessened the pain a little as I tingled in anticipation.

'Ruben and Luke Kennedy,' Ruben said to an official.

He looked up and down the page he held and licked his finger to turn it. 'Ah, here it is. There's been a mistake.'

No! I thought.

'You aren't on this flight,' he went on.

Fuck, was all my mind could say.

'What? We have to get home. Look how bad he is, we have to go home!' Ruben fumed, using my state of health as a card up his sleeve.

'I'm sorry, this flight is full. Your flight leaves in four hours.'

Four hours felt like an eternity; we were so close to heading home. I felt depleted. I had conserved all my strength and energy to make this flight and did the only thing I could do: I got out of my chair and lay on the floor with my leg up on our suitcase, a position that reduced all the pain and took the pressure off my tail bone.

Ruben left me alone to go to the pub. All he could do was drown his sorrows with the last of our money.

Damn, we were unlucky not to get on that plane. We would be in the air now. Arrgghh, there's my thoughts. Anzan said I'd recognise them more but what is recognising them: my mind or the pure me? Fuck, that's confusing.

Just don't stress about it, I heard Anzan's voice say.

Fuck, there's another voice in my head. This is insane. My mind is fucked. Wait, Anzan said it would be like this. Just chill.

Although I was lying on the floor I had a good view of the lobby, so I people watched to stay the boredom. Sitting across from where I was a young teenaged Thai boy was making hand gestures at a man seated next to him. The man started with his own gestures before I realised they were using sign language. The man caught me looking and smiled.

'What happened to you, sir?' he said loudly over the crowd of people. Before I could answer he continued speaking but I couldn't hear him for all the noise.

As exhausted as I was, something compelled me to get up and speak with these two.

'Hi, I'm Luke,' I introduced myself, shaking both their hands.

'Hi, Luke,' the father said, before doing sign language to the boy.

'Hellow,' the boy said to me in the deep voice common to deaf people.

'I had a motorbike accident,' I said.

The father immediately did sign language to the boy. 'Sorry, I know,' the boy said.

Confused, I looked to his father for an answer.

'It's how he is deaf. He was on the back of my bike when he young and we had crash. He is total deaf. From hearing now total deaf,' the father explained.

I shook my head sympathetically at the boy. He shrugged his shoulders as if to say 'Oh, well.'

'Drink, please,' the young boy said to his dad while simultaneously signing.

I heard loud laughter from behind us and turned to see a dreadlocked teen with an older man.

'Hear his voice, he sounds retarded,' I vaguely heard the teen say in between his laughter.

I glared at the man, which wiped the smile from his face. He got up and walked away. As he walked past where we sat he looked back at the deaf boy and caught his eye. The dreadlocked man gave a fake smile before putting his head down.

I looked back at the boy. Despite not being able to hear what was said he had tears in his eyes. His father grabbed at his arm but the boy shrugged free and stormed off.

'Some people very mean,' the father said, as he picked up his bags to follow his son.

'I was hardly able to hear what that guy said over all this noise. Your son is totally deaf, isn't he?' I asked.

'He is deaf, but always present. That is why he hears more than any of us.'

I was now by myself again, so I laid back down. I could see a team of flight attendants from Qantas. Three ladies and one man stood chatting among themselves before they noticed me lying on the floor.

'Hi, sir, how are you? What happened?' one of the ladies asked.

They stood in awe while I told them the whole story.

'You should write a book about it,' the male attendant stated.

'I just might,' I jokingly replied.

'Did your brother get on the first flight?' one of them asked.

'No, he is around somewhere.' I didn't want to tell them he was at the pub.

A couple of hours passed and my conversation with the attendants had run dry.

As I glanced around the airport I could see people's thoughts visible on their faces, the most prominent being that their last couple of weeks had been spent stuck in another country. Although Australians are generally tough people, we also love home. There were some broken faces in the crowd.

'Hey, bro, how're you feeling?' Ruben asked happily. I wished I could have had a drink with him to cheer me up a bit.

Before I could answer him a man's shout cut me off.

'No way, this is rubbish!' The crowd looked over as a Qantas official bent down talking to the man. Noticing that the whole crowd was now watching, the official stood up and addressed everybody.

'We are sorry, but your flight will have a stopover in Adelaide for five hours.'

I heard 100 deep breaths that were followed by slow sighs. There was a silence indicating that everybody had taken the news well enough. At least Adelaide was a step closer to home.

'At least we can say we have been to Adelaide now,' came Ruben's drunken response.

I burst out laughing: I found it incredibly funny. After all we had been through and Ruben's constant negativity, I found it hilarious that at that moment he saw optimism.

The attendant, now finished with the public announcement, walked over to us.

'Mister Kennedy, I'm sorry but we couldn't get you into business class.' I waited for this bearer of bad news to tell me more. 'However, we are breaking protocol for you by allowing you to sit in the exit seat so you can straighten your leg. Normally we need somebody fit and healthy in case of an emergency.'

'Thank you so much! I can't stay here for much longer. Thank you,' I said through a sigh of ultimate relief.

We were heading home!

Kind of.

I shoved the remainder of my painkillers into my mouth, hoping they would knock me out in time for take-off. An official had taken me to a side office so I could inject myself with my ticket home: the DVT needle.

I was exceptionally anxious about this. I wasn't afraid of needles, and getting them at the doctor's was perfectly fine. The thing was that needles were taboo. The only people who injected themselves with needles were junkies, I thought. This was firmly embedded in my mind by the adults around me, so injecting myself made me feel like I was doing something wrong. I lifted my shirt and tried to grab a chunk of fat around my lower stomach just like the doctor at the hospital had shown me. This was hard to find since I had lost a lot of weight, having not eaten properly for weeks. I stopped thinking about it. I stuck the needle in and it was done. I exited the room and felt as though I had stolen something. I just felt I had done something wrong and people would know if I acted suspiciously.

I played it cool and all was okay.

Two more planes to go and we are home, I thought. My arms were around Ruben's shoulders and those of an official as they helped me on. Once we were on the plane the official handed me one of my crutches.

'Here, are you boys okay from here?' he asked.

'Yeah, sweet,' I said. Ruben didn't respond.

Holding people up behind me as we manoeuvred ourselves to our exit row seats, Ruben remarked, 'Bro, people are fucking waiting.' He was coming down from his alcohol high and his mood made that abundantly clear.

A deep Aussie-accented man asked, 'Did you have a motorbike accident, mate?'

I smirked and nodded my head before continuing on. One of my arms was busy controlling my single crutch, while the other was wrapped around my pissed-off brother. Eventually I made it, and as I fell into my seven and a half hour torture chair I was banking on the tablets kicking in. They were my best bet to rid myself of a world of pain and disappointment and a brother whom I'd had enough of.

Ruben sank in his seat, clipped his seat belt on and was asleep before the plane was fully boarded. The plane lifted off. It smelled like a busload of camp kids – body odours, well-worn clothes, unbrushed teeth and bad breath, even stinky shoes. Every one urging us to get home to loved ones.

My leg was even more swollen, so I looked down at the nuisance thing. *I might lose this fucking thing. Wouldn't be a nuisance then!* I could feel the pus and blood mixing from the pressure on my tail bone: the drugs hadn't worked. I would have to sit this trip out. The pain made me feel sick. Singapore was gone, but pain remained.

I decided to venture to the toilets and clean myself up. 'Bro, I need to go toilet.' I nudged Ruben, but he didn't wake. I tried to shake him awake but he didn't respond. *Guess he's had enough of me too.*

I had to get to the toilet, so I stood up propped on my single crutch and used the headrest of each seat as walking aides to get me to my destination. It took a few minutes, but I made it. When the toilet door closed behind me I took a moment to rest. I was happy to be alone. I did what I had gone there for and wiped some of the pus away. The pain was soul shaking.

I glanced at myself in the mirror.

Mirrors would always bring me into the moment. I stood, transfixed.

I felt sorry for my reflection. It was as though I was witnessing somebody else going through hell. The face staring back at me had dried-up saliva in the corners of its purple, bleeding, cracked lips. Both eyes were a defeated yellow with dark red highways of veins running through them, and these eyes sat on top of heavy black bags. The unshaven beard and mustache sat out front unattended like the lawn of a derelict house full of weeds. The stitches on the chin were holding on for dear life, keeping the infection from bursting out of the obviously broken jaw.

I felt sorrier for the figure in the mirror than I did for my actual self. It was weird.

I finished cleaning up and prepped for the journey back to my seat, which felt easier than the trip to the toilet. Other people on the plane watched with grimaces as I made my way uncomfortably to my seat, my face a permanent pain-filled frown. A man shook his head at me in pity as though he was disappointed that he couldn't help my situation. Once at my seat I lowered myself slowly, and when I hit the bottom pain shot through me like I had sat on a vinegar-soaked nail. My tail bone throbbed.

We were only two hours in and I was slowly slipping back to insanity. My mind was playing tricks on me. It felt as though the chair was engulfing me, and every time someone came from behind me it felt as though they were jumping out of my head. Conversations echoed around me. I couldn't stop my eyes from popping. I tried pulling my head into my body to get away from the madness.

I pictured myself in other people's eyes and tried to act normal. Even when I was going mad I cared what others thought about me.

'You alright?' Ruben asked, suspiciously. He had woken up without me noticing.

'Yep, feel okay.' I sat up and tried to act straight. It took me back to the moments I'd do this to my mum. I'd be off my head on drugs but try to play it cool so she wouldn't suspect anything. I couldn't let her see; she would have been disappointed. Now I was evading Ruben's disappointment.

Another hour passed and my mind remained in its frenzied state. The plane felt as though it was closing in on me, and the air had become claustrophobic. I began arguing with myself, my voice echoing in my head.

Come on, let's get out of here. Jump up and let's go. Go where? Fuck that, you're just tripping out, try to sleep. No way you are going to sleep! Pull the door open, it will be better than this shit.

I stared at the hatch of the large exit doors. It had a big red line going in one direction that said 'EXIT, OPEN'.

I just sat and stared, waiting for my mind to relax. Everything had taken its toll.

Where is Anzan now? I thought. *Some saviour he is. Just chill, he said it would be a gradual thing. Fuck him. Don't say that. He's just trying to help. Think of your breathing . . .*

Another scary hour passed, and after occasionally being conscious of my breath I was doing a little better.

'Cup of tea or coffee, sir?' A beautiful lady with impeccable make-up stood next to me with a cart between her and another lady who was just as beautiful.

'No, thank you,' I managed to say.

'You know, sir, everything will work out. You will get over this and your life is going to be great. The best things in life come out of what seems the worst at the time. It allows us to appreciate living even more.'

I looked over at Ruben, who hadn't reacted to this philosophical beauty. She proceeded to the next row and I wondered whether I had imagined the whole thing. Regardless, it made me feel good. Her words about appreciating the best things after going through hard times were a lot like my own thoughts.

I call it my 'Lisa Simpson theory on life': you need the bad to appreciate the good. If things were always good then you wouldn't appreciate it as there would be no contrast. Just like the character Lisa Simpson in *The Simpsons*: she's a dull, boring character, which makes Homer even funnier so he stands out more. If the show were full of Homers there would be no contrast.

Arguing with myself once again, I came to the conclusion that I must have been imagining what the attendant said.

A few more painstaking hours had passed. 'Cabin crew prepare for landing.'

I sat up properly and tingled with excitement.

Landing in Adelaide meant we were one step away from home. As I exited the plane I passed the philosophical flight attendant, who was at the front of the plane thanking everybody for flying.

'Remember what I said,' she stated in a serious tone as I hopped past. 'What did she say?' Ruben asked from under my arm.

'Nothing much.'

We had another wait, but this one wouldn't be so bad. We were almost home.

Once we had collected our bags I found an empty patch of sunlit floor. I breathed in comfort. We were now in Australia and I felt safe. Ruben became chatty while we waited.

'Fuck, man, that shit is unheard of. I didn't think we would get out of there. We are almost home, though,' he said as he grinned at me.

The events in Thailand and beyond could have potentially ripped us apart. At times I had hated being with him and, no doubt, he had hated being with me. It definitely put our love to the test. We were struggling for life in another country. We were back in Australia and I could see the relief on Ruben's face as he opened up and told me his feelings and thoughts.

'Hey, you know I don't like talking about this kind of stuff,' Ruben attempted.

'Relax,' I butted in, knowing how hard it was for him. 'I want to say this: I got taught a few lessons on the trip about silence, but now is not the time to be silent. I love you, bro.'

With that we were both silent.

'Qantas flight to Sydney now boarding,' we heard over the loud speakers. Home stretch!

Ruben helped me up, held my arm and wrapped it around him. He carried me differently this time; I could feel the pride in his stride. We headed towards the plane to board.

'Here, sir, let me help,' a male flight attendant suggested.

'Nah, it's okay, I've got him,' Ruben said.

The plane's engines roared as we boarded. Ruben and I looked at each other. We both smiled.

'Nearly there, brother,' Ruben said. We were two hours from home and a lifetime away from Thailand.

The two hours went quickly. As we flew over Sydney I looked out of the window and tears filled my eyes. We lowered through the sky then the plane's wheels finally kissed the tarmac and skidded a little. I had wished for and imagined this exact moment for the entire trip. I didn't think we'd make it. I felt my body shut down. It knew we were home, and it knew there was no more fighting to be done.

We said goodbye to the Qantas crew and hopped off the plane, and were met by a man holding a wheelchair.

'This is for you, Mr Kennedy.'

The crowd to go through customs was as crazy as a football crowd. People were again pushing in and swearing and had lost all respect for each other.

We waited 45 minutes to reach the front of the line. The customs officers took one look at me and let us straight through without checking our bags. We couldn't take the wheelchair further than the gates, so I was back on the crutches with my arm around Ruben. I couldn't hold my own weight, so he had to help. We slowly struggled out to an expectant crowd, but there was only one face I was looking for.

'Dad?' I quietly said to myself, noticing him glaring around the room. It's all I had left. I broke down and collapsed on the floor. He rushed over, picked me up and gave me the biggest hug I had ever received.

He didn't say a word. I could feel him silently sobbing a little through his breath. His warmth and soft cotton jumper comforted me more than I had ever been comforted in my whole life.

'Dad,' I said through my tears.

'Shhh.'

ABOUT THE AUTHOR

Luke Kennedy, one of Australia's most sought-after public speakers, uses his personal story to inspire profound, lasting change and self-awareness for a wide range of audiences, from primary and high schools to businesses, special events and even prisons.

For eight years of his life Luke was an obese alcoholic and drug-addicted thug. He led a violent street-fighting crew and was stabbed on two separate occasions: once in his lung and the other time in his head. On the outside he looked strong and confident, even happy at times, but on the inside his thoughts haunted him. He was incredibly scared, depressed, anxious and paranoid and was obsessed with what others thought about him.

After losing 50 kilos Luke turned his life around through the disciplines of sport as a state champion boxer and business, and also through a constant desire to progress in every area of life: spiritually, emotionally, mentally and physically. Along with being a motivational speaker he is an author, mental health advocate and mentor to troubled youth.

www.lukeskennedy.com